The Musician's Practice Log

The Musician's Practice Log

Burton Kaplan

- **Practice Time Management Sheet**
- **Daily Practice Organizer**
- **Daily Practice Log and Weekly Summaries**
- **Weekly and Monthly Reflections**
- **Practice Profile Graphs**
- **Diary of Ideas**
- **Technique, Repertoire, and Performance Achievement Sheets**
- **Guide to Types of Practicing**

 **Perception Development Techniques,** NEW YORK

ISBN-13: 978-0-918316-04-2
ISBN-10: 0-918316-04-9

Perception Development Techniques
415 West Hill Road, Morris, NY 13808

For ordering information, call 212-662-6634
or go to
www.magicmountainmusic.org

to the practicer

For many of us, practicing is a tedious, a frustrating, and too often a boring activity. Why then do so many do it? Probably because making music on an instrument is a wonderfully joyous and fulfilling activity when you can finally play a piece through without strain.

As a practicer myself, I've been searching for ways to make practicing a more satisfying experience. I feel that the entire experience should be meaningful, not just the moment when you finally have control of the piece you've been studying for a month. I created The Musician's Practice Log to help you to achieve such satisfaction. Using the MPL, you will discover how you can use your time more effectively. You will find that once you have a clear record of what you are doing in your practicing, you will have ideas of your own for making effective changes. In addition, the information in your log will enable your teacher to give you specific advice on how to make your practicing a more creative and rewarding activity.

I have designed the log so that it will take you only five to ten minutes each day to fill it in. You will collect three kinds of information: (1) the time you put in on each piece or exercise; (2) the ideas and feelings that you have while you practice; (3) your reflections on your practicing at the end of each week and month.

You will collect the information you enter in your log on Practice Profile Graphs. As the weeks go by, these graphs will provide a picture of your practicing efforts, and you will begin to see patterns in your work. For example: the graph below has been filled in once a week for 8 weeks.

2. As I practiced, I (rarely, sometimes, often) succumbed to distractions.

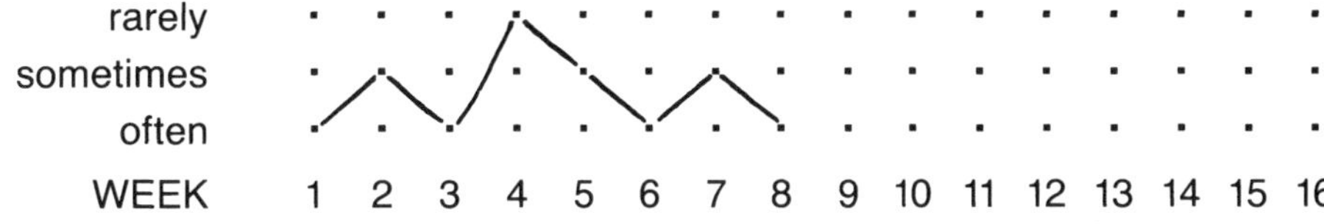

Each week, the practicer above has extended the line to the dot which best expresses his response to the statement. This graph shows that this practicer has been easily distracted while practicing. If you put in regular practice time, but are frequently distracted from what you are doing, your concentration will be poor and your "hard work" will not pay off. Once the problem is defined, however, you will be able to do something about it.

The example on the preceding page illustrates one of the many features of the MPL which can help you to increase your satisfaction as a practicer. I suggest that you thumb through the MPL now to get the feel of it. Then turn to page 5 and read the section on "how to use this book."

As you use The Musician's Practice Log, you will be guided on a voyage of self-discovery which is both fascinating and useful. As with all voyages into the unknown, it will require your courage and strength.

Bon Voyage, fellow practicer,

Burton Kaplan

to the teacher

If we as music teachers could guide our students daily, as athletic coaches guide young athletes, our students would progress faster, more efficiently, and more comfortably than at present. Unfortunately, our students are their own coaches six days a week. The doors of their practice rooms are closed, for all practical purposes, and we know little of what actually occurs there.

The Musician's Practice Log opens the practice room door wide enough to enable you to guide your students during their practice in a way previously impossible. The MPL makes it easy for your students to keep a record of the total time they put in, how much time they allocate to each assigned item, and how effectively they use their time. A review of this practice record during their lesson will give you an inside view of their practicing, a view that will help explain what is keeping them from achieving their potential. The practice record will also give you and your student a common basis for developing new ways of practicing.

In addition, as your students log in the daily events of their practicing, they will gain their own insights into the process. Confronted with a clear record of their work, they often identify the patterns which lead to success—or to failure. In other words, the log helps them coach themselves more effectively.

Many students are quite surprised to find that they follow a pattern like this one:

PIECE OR EXERCISE: Jazz Polonaise

	Day 1	2	3	4	5	6	7
Time	0	15 min.	0	30 min.	0	10 min.	2 hrs.
Improvement		NC		PSI		NC	DLF
ideas and feelings	30 minutes gave me enough time to really get into this piece. I like it. Next week I'm going to try to do a minimum of 30 min. a day.						

WEEKLY SUMMARY	Feelings (F)	Degree of Completion (4)	Stuck Without Teacher ( )	Tempo of Consistent Control $\quad \quad = 80$

What frequently motivates the two-hour session in the pattern above is a realization, as the next lesson approaches, that little practicing has occurred. Students often practice in the same way that they write a term paper. They put it off and try to cram in all the work at the last minute. But we know — and even they know, when they stop to reflect — that such a pattern does not lead to success in learning a musical instrument. Successful habits of body coordination are not formed when practice is irregular. They are formed only as a result of daily repetition.

A completed MPL provides the concrete information you need to diagnose your students' failures to realize their potential. It enables you, therefore, to give each student custom-tailored advice that is specifically designed to help them improve their future practice.

Detailed instructions for using the MPL begin on the next page. I recommend, however, that you first look through the log casually. Then read the instructions in detail to find out how it has been designed to meet the needs of both you and your students.

B.K.
1985

how to use this book

Practice Time Management Sheet & Daily Practice Organizer

You will find the Practice Time Management Sheet & Daily Practice Organizer on opposite sides of the card that has been inserted between the pages of the Log. The card is coated with plastic so that you can use it over and over again. Write on it with a felt-tip pen. If your pen is a permanent marker, you can erase it with a paper towel dampened with alcohol. If your pen is not a permanent marker, you can erase it with a paper towel dampened with water.

I – Using the Practice Time Management Sheet

In order to practice regularly without strain, it is essential that you treat each practice session as a scheduled appointment. Just as you would not miss a scheduled class, a business meeting, or an appointment with the dentist, you must not miss your practice appointment with yourself. Use the Practice Time Management Sheet to make practice appointments in advance for an entire week. The illustration below shows how each feature should be used.

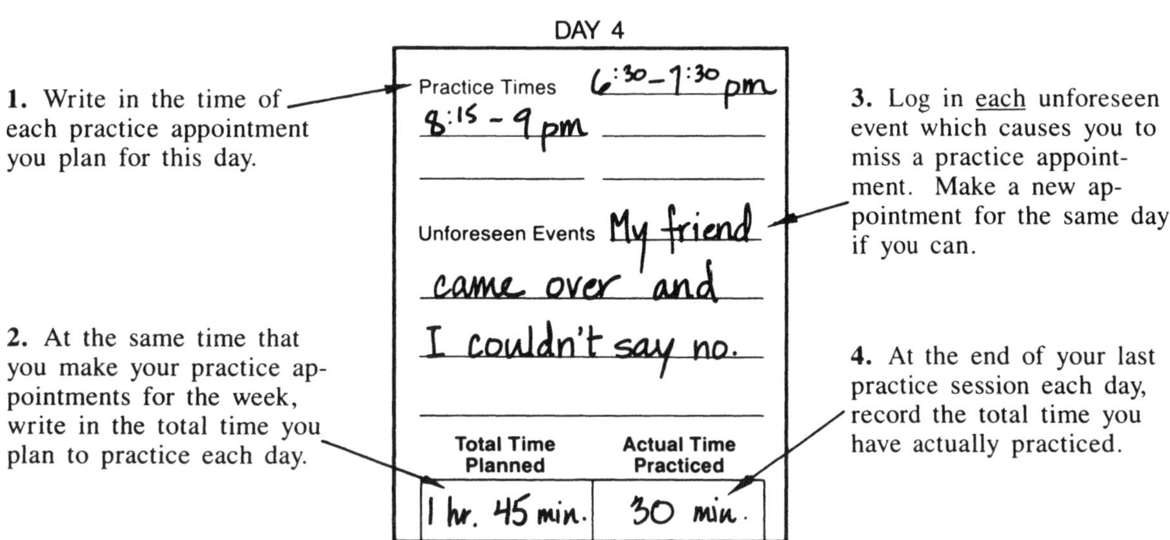

1. Write in the time of each practice appointment you plan for this day.

2. At the same time that you make your practice appointments for the week, write in the total time you plan to practice each day.

3. Log in each unforeseen event which causes you to miss a practice appointment. Make a new appointment for the same day if you can.

4. At the end of your last practice session each day, record the total time you have actually practiced.

No matter how hard you try, it is impossible to <u>always</u> practice as much as you plan to. It is essential, however, that the <u>pattern</u> of your efforts be regular and that you learn to manage your practice appointments well enough to satisfy whatever goals you have for making music. If you plan in advance each week and record the results on the "practice profile graphs" on pages 52–54, you will accumulate information that will help you manage your practice time more effectively. You can consider yourself an excellent manager of your practice time when the "actual time practiced" is the same as or more than the "total time planned" 90% of the time.

On the day before your lesson, determine the average time you <u>planned</u> for each day. At the bottom of the Practice Time Management Sheet, you will find a section to help you make your calculations.

II – Using the Daily Practice Organizer

Usually we have a limited amount of time available for our daily practice, and several pieces and exercises to cover. If we do not plan the amount of time we will spend on each item, we can easily devote so much time to one that there is little or no time for the others. Unfortunately, practicing impulsively may result in putting in a lot of time and yet mastering none of the material. Only daily repetition of a piece results in the kind of automatic control which gives us satisfaction and pride in our work. If you follow the instructions given below for using the Daily Practice Organizer, you will become a more effective practicer.

1. Decide which assigned pieces and exercises are most important and write them in here. Be sure to cover each of them every day.

Daily Practice Organizer

TOTAL TIME AVAILABLE TODAY: ___1___ Hours ___30___ Minutes

CURRENT PRIORITIES: 1 _B♭ M Scale_ 2 _Etude #3_ 3 _Serenade_

ORDER OF PRACTICE (List each Piece or Exercise)	AMOUNT OF TIME PLANNED	TYPE OF PRACTICING AND STRATEGIES PLANNED
1. B♭ Major scale — 3 octaves	15 min.	Refining — Aim: even flowing notes ♩ = 50. Keep fingers relaxed.

3. Write in here the amount of time you plan to practice each item. Give the most time to those items in which you have the least automatic control.

4. Based on your experience in today's practice, identify the type of practicing you need to do tomorrow and list any strategies you know which will help you gain control. If you are not used to making this kind of plan, turn to The Guide to Types of Practicing on page 78 for help.

2. List the items you plan to practice here. Be sure to include your current priorities as the first three items to be practiced. For the sake of variety, you may want to vary the order in which you practice them.

Principles for organizing your daily practice

1. For your practicing to pay off, you must practice each piece or exercise daily until you have automatic control — that is, until your fingers seem to play without your conscious guidance.

2. Each consecutive day you practice the same material, your control over it increases. However, your control of each piece or exercise does not grow at the same rate. Therefore, after each day's practice, make a new plan for the next practice, so that you give the most time to those pieces and passages in which you have the least automatic control.

3. It is best to practice each item every day. If you have a different amount of time available each day, divide that time so that you spend some time on each item. Until you have automatic control, you can expect to lose what you have gained one day if you do not practice the same items the next day as well.

4. On days when you have very little time available for practicing, be sure to cover at least your "current priorities."

5. If you plan to play through an entire piece or exercise, be sure to plan for the time it takes just to play through it as well as the time you will need for repair work.

6. There may be times when your practicing of a particular piece or exercise is going so well that you feel like making an impulsive change in your plan for that day. This can certainly make sense for a day or two. If it becomes a habit, however, you should discourage it. As a habit, it will lead to incomplete training, and your development of automatic control will be slowed considerably.

The Daily Practice Log and Weekly Summaries

I – Using the Daily Practice Log

It is easy for practicing to become an activity in which we play our instruments a great deal without thinking of what we are doing. By keeping a record of the time we put in on each piece or exercise, by reflecting on how much change occurs each time we practice, and by taking time to record our feelings and thoughts, we become more aware of what is going on during our practicing, and we gain the power to make improvements.

Use the Daily Practice Log, which begins on page 18, to keep a record of your practicing. Each day, log in the time you spend on each item, the degree of improvement you observe, and any "ideas" and/or "feelings" which flit through your mind and seem meaningful. Follow the directions at the top of the next page.

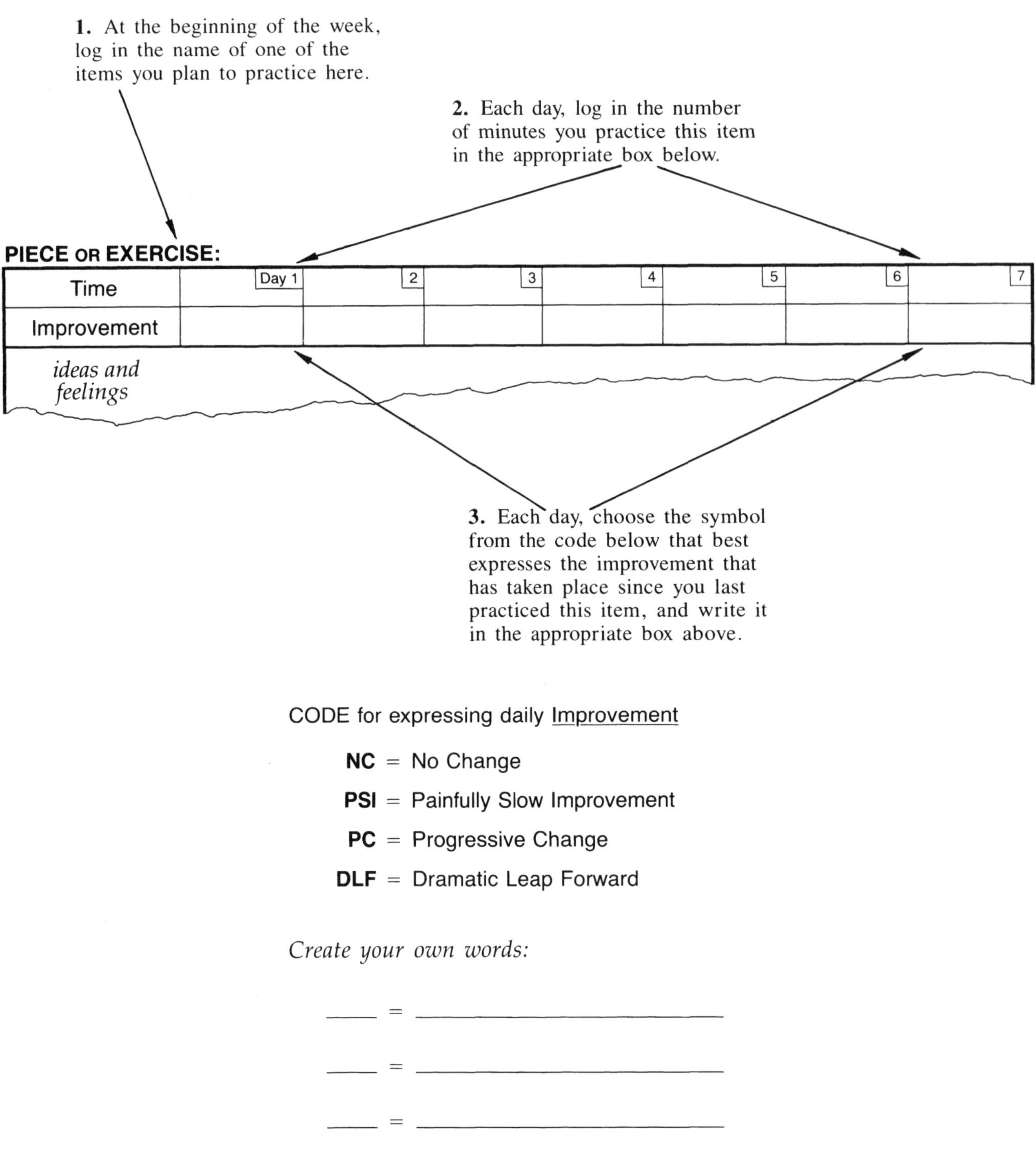

CODE for expressing daily <u>Improvement</u>

NC = No Change

PSI = Painfully Slow Improvement

PC = Progressive Change

DLF = Dramatic Leap Forward

Create your own words:

____ = ____________________

____ = ____________________

____ = ____________________

____ = ____________________

II – Using the Weekly Summaries

When we practice daily, we are so conscious of each moment that we often do not have an overall sense of the cumulative improvement which has taken place. Often our impressions are influenced by one particularly wonderful or particularly poor session which stands out in our minds. Therefore, on "Day 7," when you have finished your practice of a piece or exercise, play through it once more and evaluate the quality of your work in the summary chart which is shown at the top of the next page.

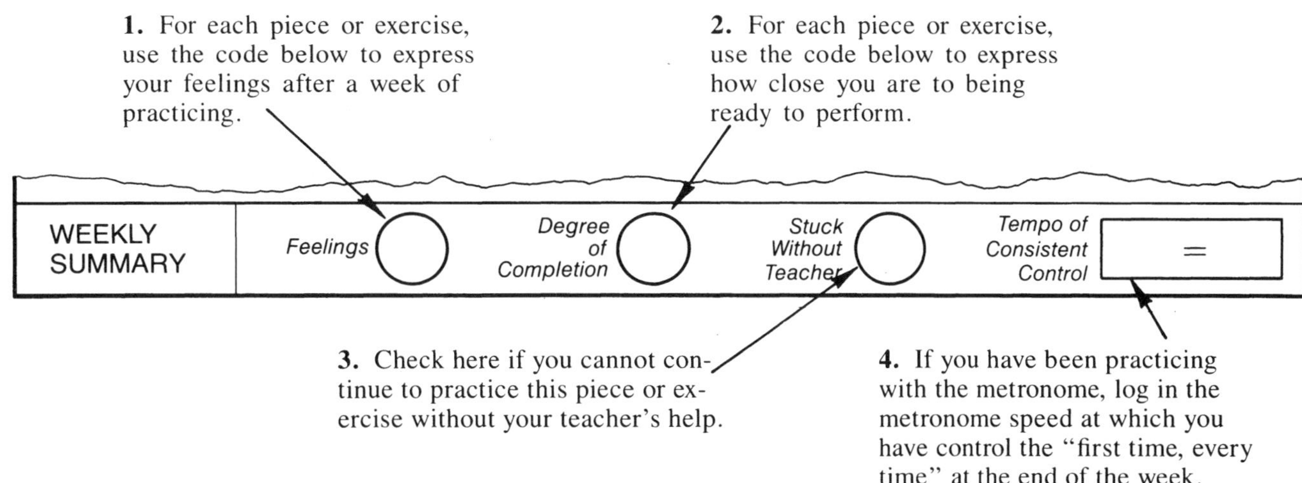

3. Check here if you cannot continue to practice this piece or exercise without your teacher's help.

4. If you have been practicing with the metronome, log in the metronome speed at which you have control the "first time, every time" at the end of the week.

CODE for expressing Feelings

   B = Bored

   F = Frustrated

SG = Satisfaction Growing

   P = Proud

   E = Ecstatic

CODE for expressing *Degree of Completion*

Use a number from 1 to 10.

   1 = just getting started

10 = ready to perform

Use decimals to express subtle changes — for example: 5.7, 5.9.

At the end of one week, the first section of your log might look like this:

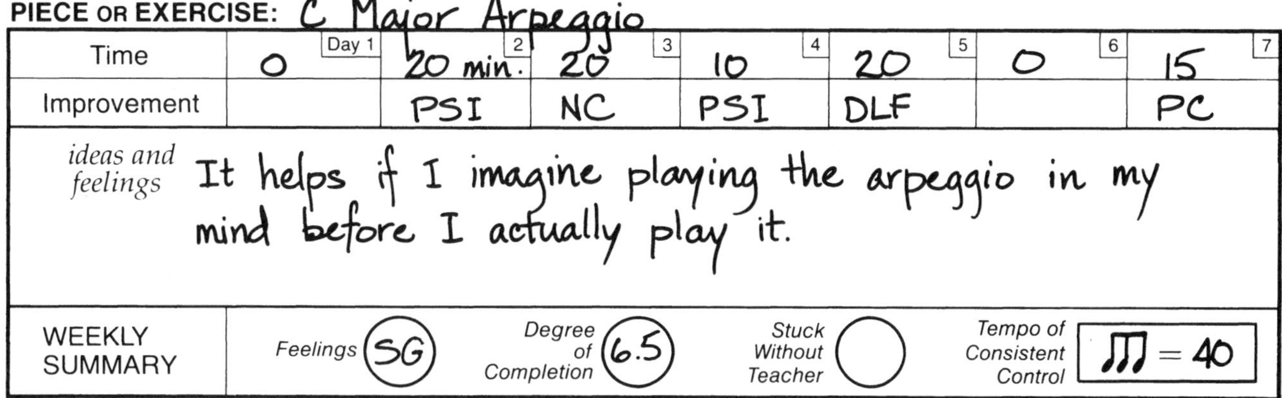

On the day before your lesson, calculate your average daily practice for the week, as shown in the illustration below. You will find boxes to help you with your calculations at the end of the Daily Practice Log sheet for each week.

Total Hrs. Practiced ÷ Total Days Available = Average Practice Per Day

An "Available Day" is a day you could have practiced if you had planned your time well. Do not count a day as available if you had not planned to practice because it was to be a day off. Include all days, however, when unforeseen events occurred, except for illness.

You should keep in mind that <u>one</u> <u>poor</u> <u>week</u> <u>of</u> practicing <u>has</u> <u>little</u> <u>impact</u> <u>on</u> <u>your</u> <u>development</u>. It is only the <u>pattern</u>, or profile, of your development over a period of two or more months that <u>reveals</u> <u>who</u> <u>you</u> <u>are</u> <u>as</u> <u>a</u> <u>practicer</u>. So, fill in everything exactly as it happens. This will provide the starting point for understanding yourself as a practicer. If your records are complete and accurate, you will be able to make intelligent decisions about improving your work.

You may find that you do not feel comfortable with your practice profile because what you actually do does not match your idea of yourself. It is your choice whether or not to hide from this knowledge. When you hide from this knowledge, you are losing an opportunity to develop your abilities. When you confront this knowledge, though it may be painful, you free yourself to grow, and grow, and grow...

Weekly and Monthly Reflections

The Reflections section is divided into two parts: 1) Putting in the Time, and 2) Using Practice Time Effectively. There is a reason for listing the parts in this order. If you are not putting in the time regularly, or if you are not putting in enough time to achieve your musical goals, the question of how effectively you use your practice time is not relevant. If you are not putting in the time regularly, your attention will wander, and you will experience the futility of trying to attain consistent automatic control without regular repetition. After several weeks, you will find that, even though the total time you've invested may seem like a lot, your expectations have not been realized. Only regular work results in <u>consistent</u> <u>automatic</u> <u>control</u>.

I – Using the Practice Profile Graphs for Putting in the Time

"Putting in the Time — weekly reflections" on pages 52–57 contains four parts which should be filled in <u>before</u> your lesson: (1) Profile of actual time practiced <u>each</u> <u>day</u>, (2) Time management profiles, (3) Profile of average daily practice <u>each</u> <u>week</u>, and (4) the Diary of Ideas.

As you extend the line in each graph week by week, a picture, or "profile," will form of how much and how regularly you've practiced. At the end of each month, you can use your profile to reflect on how satisfied you are with the time you are putting in, and to plan for improvements.

1. Profile of actual time practiced each day

After you have added up the "actual time practiced" at the end of each practice session and inserted it in the space provided on the Practice Time Management Sheet, draw it as a solid line into the appropriate Daily Profile on page 52, as shown in the illustration at the top of the next page.

In addition, use a different kind of line (dotted or colored) to show the "total time planned" for practicing each day. Your "practice profile graph" will then enable you to compare your dream ("total time planned") with reality ("actual time practiced").

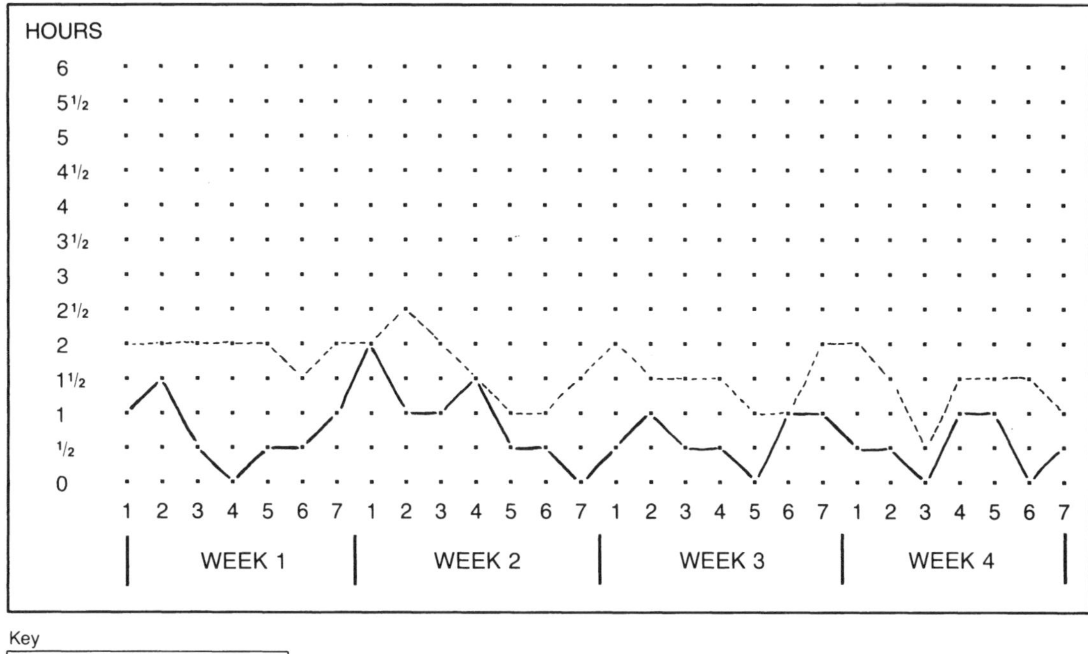

2. Time Management Profiles

These graphs will help you keep a record of how your feelings about the time you put in shift from week to week. Here is an example.

Complete these statements at the end of each week, extending the line to the dot that represents your response.

1. I practiced (more than, as much as, less than) I planned to.

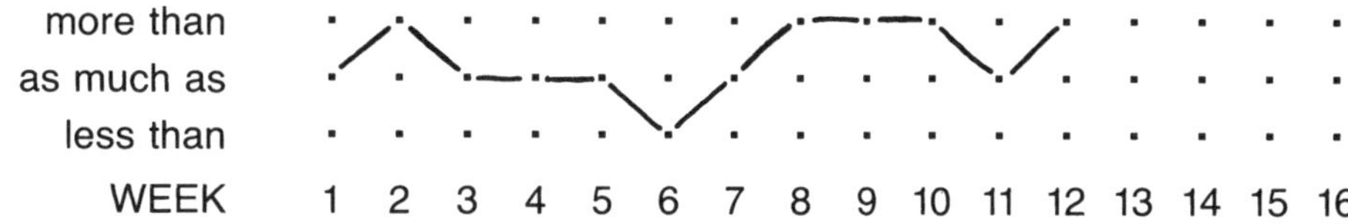

The profile above is excellent. This person practiced as much as or more than planned except during "week #6." In other words, the <u>pattern</u> is excellent though the result is <u>not perfect</u>. Sometimes students feel down because one week of work is not at their best level. It is important to have realistic expectations about a process like practicing, since it depends upon so many factors which we cannot completely control— unforeseen visitors, urgent telephone calls, illness, moods, etc.

On the other hand, the profile below is erratic.   A profile like this is worth improving.

1. I practiced (more than, as much as, less than) I planned to.

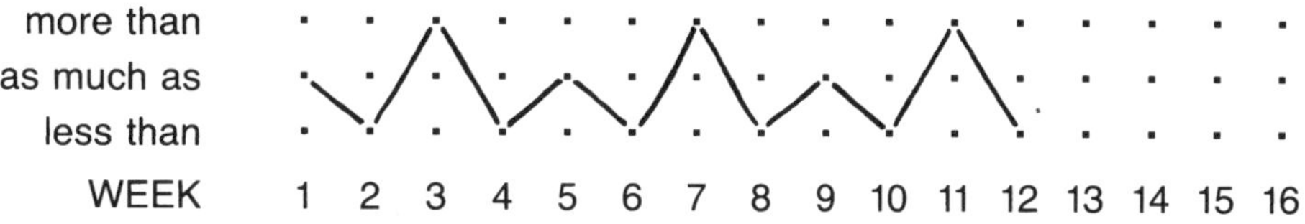

3. Profile of average daily practice each week

After you have calculated your "average practice per day" at the end of each Daily Practice Log and Weekly Summaries sheet in the section which begins on page 18, transfer it as a solid line to your weekly profile on page 54, as shown in the illustration below.

As before, use a different kind of line (dotted or colored) to show the average daily practice you <u>planned</u>. You will have calculated the "average daily time planned for the week" at the bottom of the Practice Time Management Sheet.

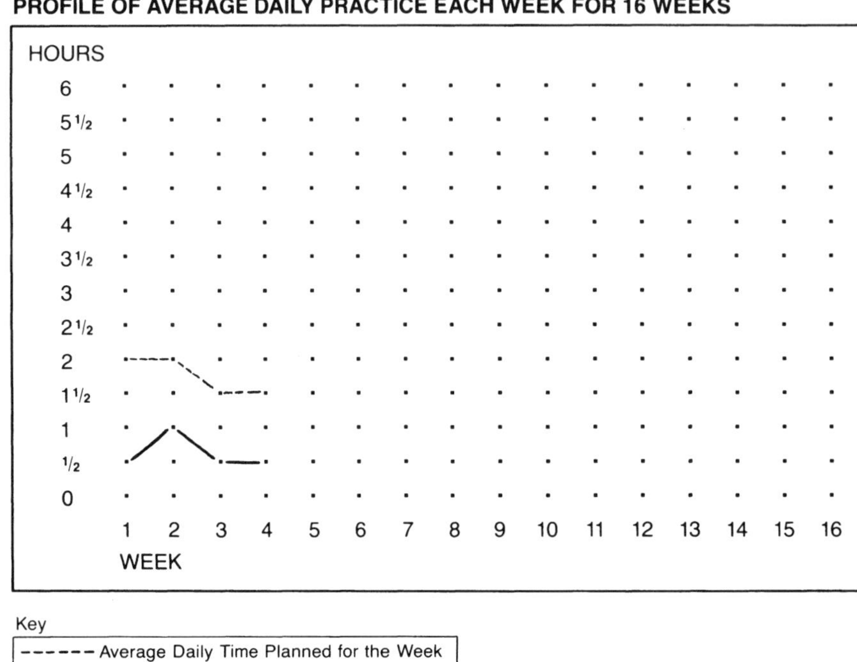

4. The Diary of Ideas

Whenever you have difficulty putting in practice time, you should take time to reflect on what you might do to improve your efforts. Record your ideas for improvement in the Diary of Ideas on pages 55–57. An example is shown below.

WK #	DATE	DIARY OF IDEAS: *How I can put in more time.*
3	2/17/85	I'm going to stop answering the phone when I practice so I can practice without interruptions. I never realized that I was …

At the end of <u>each month</u>, review your "practice profile graphs" for Putting in the Time. Use the Monthly Reflections sheets on pages 58–61 to help you reflect on how successful you have been at putting in the time.

II – Practice Profile Graphs for Using Practice Time Effectively

"Using Practice Time Effectively — weekly reflections" on pages 62–67 contains two parts which should be filled in <u>before</u> your lesson: (1) Practice Effectiveness Profiles, and (2) the Diary of Ideas.

1. Practice Effectiveness Profiles

The Practice Effectiveness Profiles on pages 62 and 63 will help you reflect about attitudes and experiences which are central in everyone's practicing, such as the degree to which you are distracted, the quality of your concentration, and whether you follow through with the training of each item until it is mastered or flit from one item to another without design. The illustration below shows you how to complete these graphs.

Complete these statements at the end of each week, extending the line to the dot that represents your response.

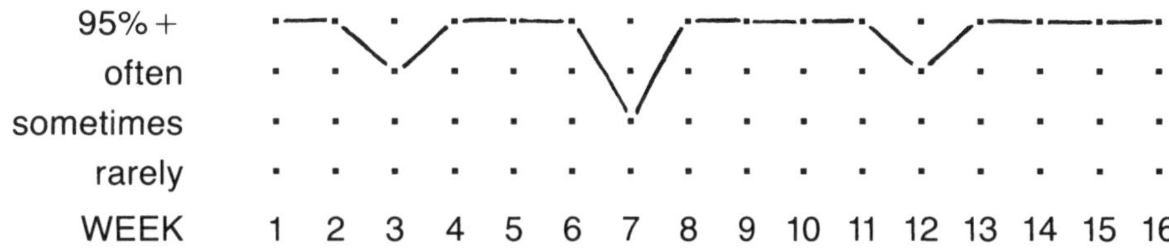

The profile above shows an excellent pattern of concentration and attention over a 16-week period. Remember, it is the <u>pattern</u> of your profile that matters, <u>not its absolute perfection</u>.

If the pattern of your concentration and attention has been erratic, your profile might look like this:

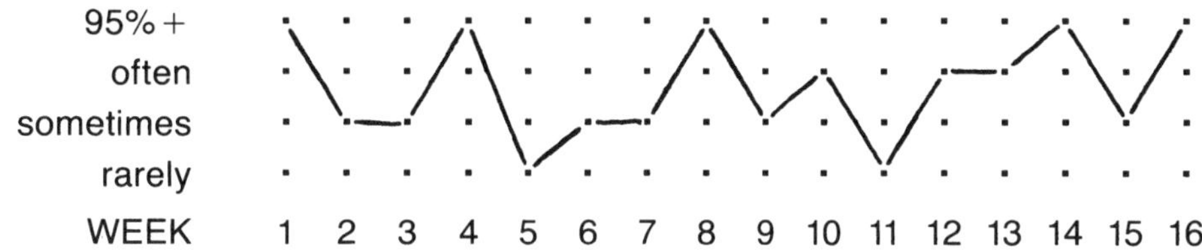

2. The Diary of Ideas

Whenever your response to one of the statements about using your practice time effectively is less than "95% +," as in Weeks #2, #3, #5, #6, and #7 in the graph above, you should take time to reflect on what you might do to improve that aspect of your practice effectiveness. Record your ideas for improvement in the "Diary of Ideas" on pages 63–67, as shown at the top of the next page.

WK #	DATE	**DIARY OF IDEAS:** *How I can improve my practice effectiveness.*
5	3/3/85	I was so happy with the strength of my concentration this week. It makes an enormous difference when I love the piece I'm studying. I'm going to speak with

At the end of <u>each</u> <u>month</u>, review your Practice Effectiveness Profiles. Use the Monthly Reflections sheets on pages 68–71 to help you reflect on how effective your practicing has been.

The Technique Achievement Summary, the Repertoire Achievement Summary, and the Record of Performances

So far, The Musician's Practice Log has provided space for recording information about the <u>process</u> of practicing. It is more usual to keep track of the <u>products</u> of work, i.e., the scales, arpeggios, etudes, and pieces which we have mastered. You will find charts on pages 72–75 that will help you keep track of your achievements.

I – The Technique Achievement Summary

Each time you complete your study of a scale, arpeggio, or etude, you should log it into the Technique Achievement Summary on pages 72 and 73.

There are two types of charts for scales and arpeggios, one for the "first level of quality," and the other for "refining quality." This distinction is made for the following reasons: (1) there are a very large number of scales and arpeggios to learn; (2) it takes years before you can play a scale or arpeggio at many different tempos, well articulated, with a beautiful tone, in tune, with 95% consistency. It is important, therefore, to recognize that you need to build your level of quality gradually, in a series of steps. That is, you should <u>not</u> perfect scales or arpeggios one at a time. Instead, first learn the notes with a 75% or 80% accuracy of intonation, tone, and articulation, at a slow tempo. Then record your accomplishment on the appropriate "first level of quality" chart. In this way you will recognize your initial work as an achievement, i.e., worthy of recognition even though not completed forever. Now go on to the next scale or arpeggio and bring it to the same level. When you have a repertoire of three or four scales or arpeggios mastered to the "first level of quality," choose one of them to refine to a higher level of quality. At the same time, add a new one to your repertoire, practicing it to the "first level of quality."

One of the greatest stumbling blocks in developing technical ability occurs when a practicer aims for technical perfection too soon. The human system is not capable of achieving 100% control 100% of the time. By building your control in a series of steps, each a refinement of the step before, you rid yourself of an impossible burden.

II – The Repertoire Achievement Summary

Each time you stop practicing a piece of music you should log it into the Repertoire Achievement Summary on page 74 and indicate the level of completion you have reached.

There are many reasons why we discontinue practicing a piece. Sometimes it is because it is at a performance level, i.e., finished. Here are some other reasons: (1) EFN—enough for now; (2) TPTL—to present technical level; (3) CSIAM—can't stand it any more. You will find a code to express these and other reasons below the Repertoire Achievement Summary on page 74. If you discontinue practicing a piece for a reason not listed, express it in your own words. You should be clear at all times whether or not the piece you have "completed" is in your repertoire (ready to perform on short notice) or is, in fact, still in the process of work but not being practiced currently. When you put a piece aside before it is in your repertoire, you are, in effect, treating it as completed to a "first level of quality." You should eventually return to it to refine it further.

III – The Record of Performances

The Record of Performances on page 75 will help you keep track of your performances.

Daily Practice Log
and Weekly Summaries

week 1

PIECE OR EXERCISE:

Time	Day 1	2	3	4	5	6	7
Improvement							

ideas and feelings

WEEKLY SUMMARY	*Feelings* ◯	*Degree of Completion* ◯	*Stuck Without Teacher* ◯	*Tempo of Consistent Control* =

PIECE OR EXERCISE:

Time	Day 1	2	3	4	5	6	7
Improvement							

ideas and feelings

WEEKLY SUMMARY	*Feelings* ◯	*Degree of Completion* ◯	*Stuck Without Teacher* ◯	*Tempo of Consistent Control* =

PIECE OR EXERCISE:

Time	Day 1	2	3	4	5	6	7
Improvement							

ideas and feelings

WEEKLY SUMMARY	*Feelings* ◯	*Degree of Completion* ◯	*Stuck Without Teacher* ◯	*Tempo of Consistent Control* =

PIECE OR EXERCISE:

Time	Day 1	2	3	4	5	6	7
Improvement							

ideas and feelings

WEEKLY SUMMARY	*Feelings* ◯	*Degree of Completion* ◯	*Stuck Without Teacher* ◯	*Tempo of Consistent Control* =

PIECE OR EXERCISE:

Time	Day 1	2	3	4	5	6	7
Improvement							

ideas and feelings

WEEKLY SUMMARY	Feelings ◯	Degree of Completion ◯	Stuck Without Teacher ◯	Tempo of Consistent Control =

PIECE OR EXERCISE:

Time	Day 1	2	3	4	5	6	7
Improvement							

ideas and feelings

WEEKLY SUMMARY	Feelings ◯	Degree of Completion ◯	Stuck Without Teacher ◯	Tempo of Consistent Control =

PIECE OR EXERCISE:

Time	Day 1	2	3	4	5	6	7
Improvement							

ideas and feelings

WEEKLY SUMMARY	Feelings ◯	Degree of Completion ◯	Stuck Without Teacher ◯	Tempo of Consistent Control =

AVERAGE DAILY PRACTICE FOR THE WEEK

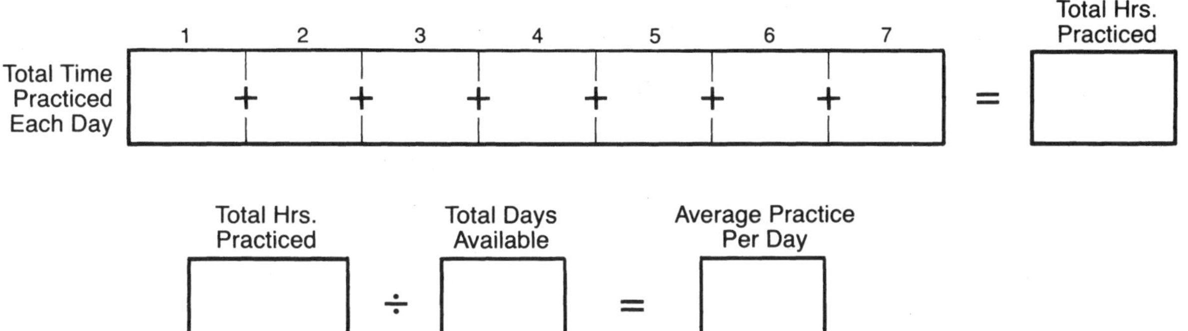

week 2

PIECE OR EXERCISE:

Time	Day 1	2	3	4	5	6	7
Improvement							

ideas and feelings

WEEKLY SUMMARY	Feelings ◯	Degree of Completion ◯	Stuck Without Teacher ◯	Tempo of Consistent Control =

PIECE OR EXERCISE:

Time	Day 1	2	3	4	5	6	7
Improvement							

ideas and feelings

WEEKLY SUMMARY	Feelings ◯	Degree of Completion ◯	Stuck Without Teacher ◯	Tempo of Consistent Control =

PIECE OR EXERCISE:

Time	Day 1	2	3	4	5	6	7
Improvement							

ideas and feelings

WEEKLY SUMMARY	Feelings ◯	Degree of Completion ◯	Stuck Without Teacher ◯	Tempo of Consistent Control =

PIECE OR EXERCISE:

Time	Day 1	2	3	4	5	6	7
Improvement							

ideas and feelings

WEEKLY SUMMARY	Feelings ◯	Degree of Completion ◯	Stuck Without Teacher ◯	Tempo of Consistent Control =

PIECE OR EXERCISE:

Time	Day 1	2	3	4	5	6	7
Improvement							

ideas and feelings

WEEKLY SUMMARY	Feelings ◯	Degree of Completion ◯	Stuck Without Teacher ◯	Tempo of Consistent Control	=

PIECE OR EXERCISE:

Time	Day 1	2	3	4	5	6	7
Improvement							

ideas and feelings

WEEKLY SUMMARY	Feelings ◯	Degree of Completion ◯	Stuck Without Teacher ◯	Tempo of Consistent Control	=

PIECE OR EXERCISE:

Time	Day 1	2	3	4	5	6	7
Improvement							

ideas and feelings

WEEKLY SUMMARY	Feelings ◯	Degree of Completion ◯	Stuck Without Teacher ◯	Tempo of Consistent Control	=

AVERAGE DAILY PRACTICE FOR THE WEEK

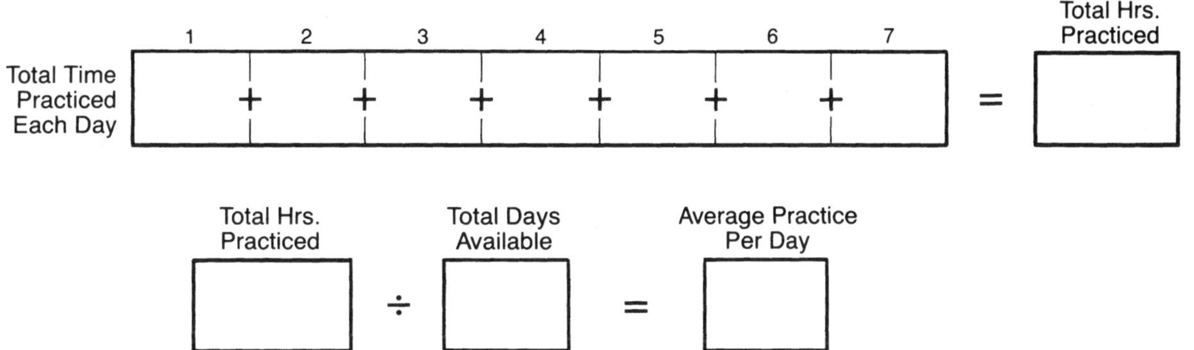

week 3

PIECE OR EXERCISE:

Time	Day 1	2	3	4	5	6	7
Improvement							

ideas and feelings

| WEEKLY SUMMARY | *Feelings* ◯ | *Degree of Completion* ◯ | *Stuck Without Teacher* ◯ | *Tempo of Consistent Control* = |

PIECE OR EXERCISE:

Time	Day 1	2	3	4	5	6	7
Improvement							

ideas and feelings

| WEEKLY SUMMARY | *Feelings* ◯ | *Degree of Completion* ◯ | *Stuck Without Teacher* ◯ | *Tempo of Consistent Control* = |

PIECE OR EXERCISE:

Time	Day 1	2	3	4	5	6	7
Improvement							

ideas and feelings

| WEEKLY SUMMARY | *Feelings* ◯ | *Degree of Completion* ◯ | *Stuck Without Teacher* ◯ | *Tempo of Consistent Control* = |

PIECE OR EXERCISE:

Time	Day 1	2	3	4	5	6	7
Improvement							

ideas and feelings

| WEEKLY SUMMARY | *Feelings* ◯ | *Degree of Completion* ◯ | *Stuck Without Teacher* ◯ | *Tempo of Consistent Control* = |

From _________ to _________ 20 __

PIECE OR EXERCISE:

Time	Day 1	2	3	4	5	6	7
Improvement							

ideas and feelings

WEEKLY SUMMARY	*Feelings* ◯	*Degree of Completion* ◯	*Stuck Without Teacher* ◯	*Tempo of Consistent Control* =

PIECE OR EXERCISE:

Time	Day 1	2	3	4	5	6	7
Improvement							

ideas and feelings

WEEKLY SUMMARY	*Feelings* ◯	*Degree of Completion* ◯	*Stuck Without Teacher* ◯	*Tempo of Consistent Control* =

PIECE OR EXERCISE:

Time	Day 1	2	3	4	5	6	7
Improvement							

ideas and feelings

WEEKLY SUMMARY	*Feelings* ◯	*Degree of Completion* ◯	*Stuck Without Teacher* ◯	*Tempo of Consistent Control* =

AVERAGE DAILY PRACTICE FOR THE WEEK

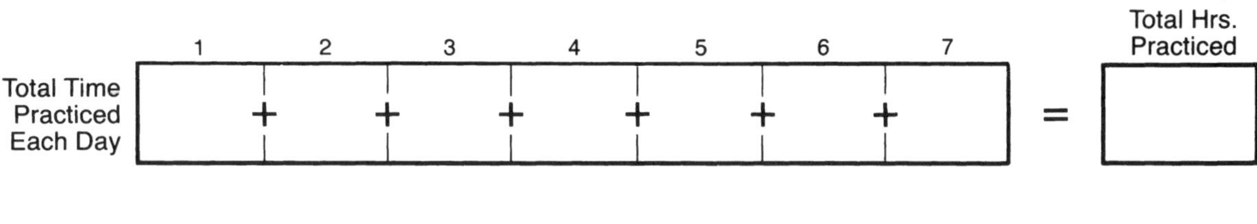

Total Time Practiced Each Day: 1 + 2 + 3 + 4 + 5 + 6 + 7 = Total Hrs. Practiced

Total Hrs. Practiced ÷ Total Days Available = Average Practice Per Day

week 4

PIECE OR EXERCISE:

Time	Day 1	2	3	4	5	6	7
Improvement							

ideas and feelings

| WEEKLY SUMMARY | *Feelings* ◯ | *Degree of Completion* ◯ | *Stuck Without Teacher* ◯ | *Tempo of Consistent Control* = |

PIECE OR EXERCISE:

Time	Day 1	2	3	4	5	6	7
Improvement							

ideas and feelings

| WEEKLY SUMMARY | *Feelings* ◯ | *Degree of Completion* ◯ | *Stuck Without Teacher* ◯ | *Tempo of Consistent Control* = |

PIECE OR EXERCISE:

Time	Day 1	2	3	4	5	6	7
Improvement							

ideas and feelings

| WEEKLY SUMMARY | *Feelings* ◯ | *Degree of Completion* ◯ | *Stuck Without Teacher* ◯ | *Tempo of Consistent Control* = |

PIECE OR EXERCISE:

Time	Day 1	2	3	4	5	6	7
Improvement							

ideas and feelings

| WEEKLY SUMMARY | *Feelings* ◯ | *Degree of Completion* ◯ | *Stuck Without Teacher* ◯ | *Tempo of Consistent Control* = |

From _______ to _______ 20 __

PIECE OR **EXERCISE:**

Time	Day 1	2	3	4	5	6	7
Improvement							

ideas and feelings

WEEKLY SUMMARY	Feelings ◯	Degree of Completion ◯	Stuck Without Teacher ◯	Tempo of Consistent Control =

PIECE OR **EXERCISE:**

Time	Day 1	2	3	4	5	6	7
Improvement							

ideas and feelings

WEEKLY SUMMARY	Feelings ◯	Degree of Completion ◯	Stuck Without Teacher ◯	Tempo of Consistent Control =

PIECE OR **EXERCISE:**

Time	Day 1	2	3	4	5	6	7
Improvement							

ideas and feelings

WEEKLY SUMMARY	Feelings ◯	Degree of Completion ◯	Stuck Without Teacher ◯	Tempo of Consistent Control =

AVERAGE DAILY PRACTICE FOR THE WEEK

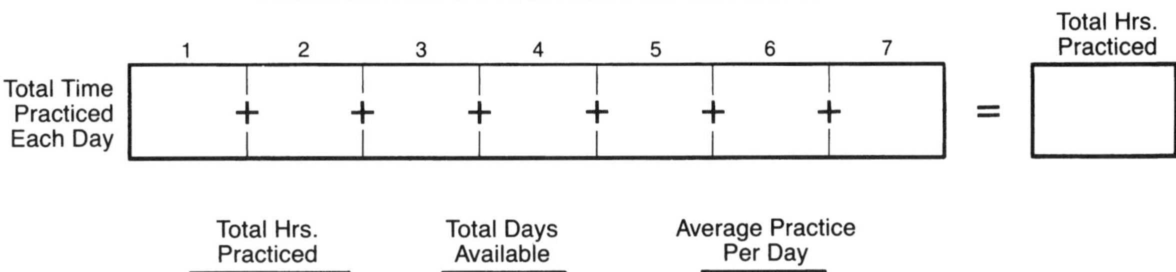

week 5

PIECE OR EXERCISE:

Time	Day 1	2	3	4	5	6	7
Improvement							

ideas and feelings

| WEEKLY SUMMARY | *Feelings* ◯ | *Degree of Completion* ◯ | *Stuck Without Teacher* ◯ | *Tempo of Consistent Control* $=$ |

PIECE OR EXERCISE:

Time	Day 1	2	3	4	5	6	7
Improvement							

ideas and feelings

| WEEKLY SUMMARY | *Feelings* ◯ | *Degree of Completion* ◯ | *Stuck Without Teacher* ◯ | *Tempo of Consistent Control* $=$ |

PIECE OR EXERCISE:

Time	Day 1	2	3	4	5	6	7
Improvement							

ideas and feelings

| WEEKLY SUMMARY | *Feelings* ◯ | *Degree of Completion* ◯ | *Stuck Without Teacher* ◯ | *Tempo of Consistent Control* $=$ |

PIECE OR EXERCISE:

Time	Day 1	2	3	4	5	6	7
Improvement							

ideas and feelings

| WEEKLY SUMMARY | *Feelings* ◯ | *Degree of Completion* ◯ | *Stuck Without Teacher* ◯ | *Tempo of Consistent Control* $=$ |

PIECE OR EXERCISE:

Time	Day 1	2	3	4	5	6	7
Improvement							

ideas and feelings

| WEEKLY SUMMARY | *Feelings* ◯ | *Degree of Completion* ◯ | *Stuck Without Teacher* ◯ | *Tempo of Consistent Control* | = |

PIECE OR EXERCISE:

Time	Day 1	2	3	4	5	6	7
Improvement							

ideas and feelings

| WEEKLY SUMMARY | *Feelings* ◯ | *Degree of Completion* ◯ | *Stuck Without Teacher* ◯ | *Tempo of Consistent Control* | = |

PIECE OR EXERCISE:

Time	Day 1	2	3	4	5	6	7
Improvement							

ideas and feelings

| WEEKLY SUMMARY | *Feelings* ◯ | *Degree of Completion* ◯ | *Stuck Without Teacher* ◯ | *Tempo of Consistent Control* | = |

AVERAGE DAILY PRACTICE FOR THE WEEK

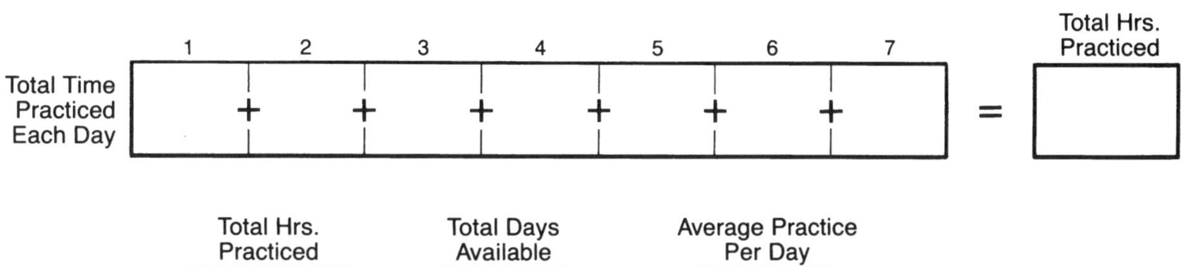

week 6

PIECE OR EXERCISE:

Time	Day 1	2	3	4	5	6	7
Improvement							

ideas and feelings

WEEKLY SUMMARY	*Feelings* ◯	*Degree of Completion* ◯	*Stuck Without Teacher* ◯	*Tempo of Consistent Control*	=

PIECE OR EXERCISE:

Time	Day 1	2	3	4	5	6	7
Improvement							

ideas and feelings

WEEKLY SUMMARY	*Feelings* ◯	*Degree of Completion* ◯	*Stuck Without Teacher* ◯	*Tempo of Consistent Control*	=

PIECE OR EXERCISE:

Time	Day 1	2	3	4	5	6	7
Improvement							

ideas and feelings

WEEKLY SUMMARY	*Feelings* ◯	*Degree of Completion* ◯	*Stuck Without Teacher* ◯	*Tempo of Consistent Control*	=

PIECE OR EXERCISE:

Time	Day 1	2	3	4	5	6	7
Improvement							

ideas and feelings

WEEKLY SUMMARY	*Feelings* ◯	*Degree of Completion* ◯	*Stuck Without Teacher* ◯	*Tempo of Consistent Control*	=

PIECE OR EXERCISE:

Time	Day 1	2	3	4	5	6	7
Improvement							

ideas and feelings

| WEEKLY SUMMARY | *Feelings* ◯ | *Degree of Completion* ◯ | *Stuck Without Teacher* ◯ | *Tempo of Consistent Control* [=] |

PIECE OR EXERCISE:

Time	Day 1	2	3	4	5	6	7
Improvement							

ideas and feelings

| WEEKLY SUMMARY | *Feelings* ◯ | *Degree of Completion* ◯ | *Stuck Without Teacher* ◯ | *Tempo of Consistent Control* [=] |

PIECE OR EXERCISE:

Time	Day 1	2	3	4	5	6	7
Improvement							

ideas and feelings

| WEEKLY SUMMARY | *Feelings* ◯ | *Degree of Completion* ◯ | *Stuck Without Teacher* ◯ | *Tempo of Consistent Control* [=] |

AVERAGE DAILY PRACTICE FOR THE WEEK

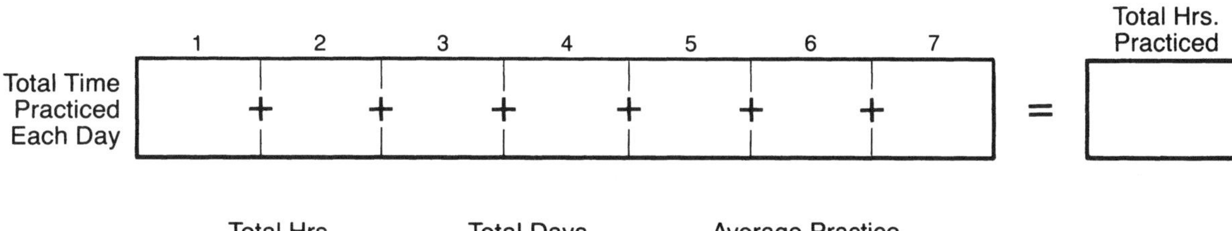

Total Time Practiced Each Day: 1 + 2 + 3 + 4 + 5 + 6 + 7 = Total Hrs. Practiced

Total Hrs. Practiced ÷ Total Days Available = Average Practice Per Day

week 7

PIECE OR EXERCISE:

Time	Day 1	2	3	4	5	6	7
Improvement							

ideas and feelings

| WEEKLY SUMMARY | *Feelings* ◯ | *Degree of Completion* ◯ | *Stuck Without Teacher* ◯ | *Tempo of Consistent Control* | = |

PIECE OR EXERCISE:

Time	Day 1	2	3	4	5	6	7
Improvement							

ideas and feelings

| WEEKLY SUMMARY | *Feelings* ◯ | *Degree of Completion* ◯ | *Stuck Without Teacher* ◯ | *Tempo of Consistent Control* | = |

PIECE OR EXERCISE:

Time	Day 1	2	3	4	5	6	7
Improvement							

ideas and feelings

| WEEKLY SUMMARY | *Feelings* ◯ | *Degree of Completion* ◯ | *Stuck Without Teacher* ◯ | *Tempo of Consistent Control* | = |

PIECE OR EXERCISE:

Time	Day 1	2	3	4	5	6	7
Improvement							

ideas and feelings

| WEEKLY SUMMARY | *Feelings* ◯ | *Degree of Completion* ◯ | *Stuck Without Teacher* ◯ | *Tempo of Consistent Control* | = |

PIECE OR **EXERCISE:**

Time	Day 1	2	3	4	5	6	7
Improvement							

ideas and feelings

| WEEKLY SUMMARY | Feelings ◯ | Degree of Completion ◯ | Stuck Without Teacher ◯ | Tempo of Consistent Control | = |

PIECE OR **EXERCISE:**

Time	Day 1	2	3	4	5	6	7
Improvement							

ideas and feelings

| WEEKLY SUMMARY | Feelings ◯ | Degree of Completion ◯ | Stuck Without Teacher ◯ | Tempo of Consistent Control | = |

PIECE OR **EXERCISE:**

Time	Day 1	2	3	4	5	6	7
Improvement							

ideas and feelings

| WEEKLY SUMMARY | Feelings ◯ | Degree of Completion ◯ | Stuck Without Teacher ◯ | Tempo of Consistent Control | = |

AVERAGE DAILY PRACTICE FOR THE WEEK

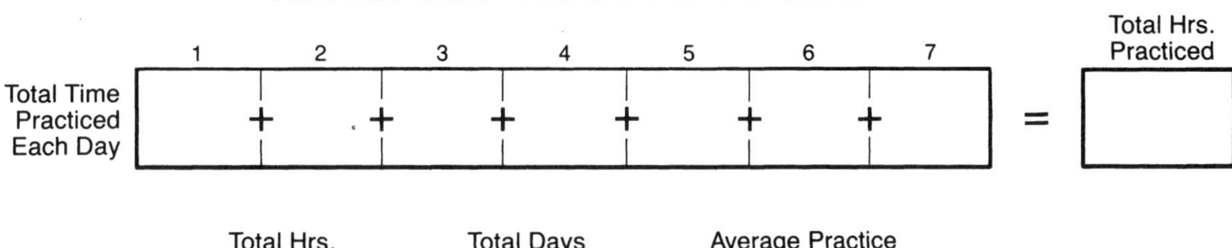

week 8

PIECE OR EXERCISE:

Time	Day 1	2	3	4	5	6	7
Improvement							

ideas and feelings

| WEEKLY SUMMARY | *Feelings* ◯ | *Degree of Completion* ◯ | *Stuck Without Teacher* ◯ | *Tempo of Consistent Control* | = |

PIECE OR EXERCISE:

Time	Day 1	2	3	4	5	6	7
Improvement							

ideas and feelings

| WEEKLY SUMMARY | *Feelings* ◯ | *Degree of Completion* ◯ | *Stuck Without Teacher* ◯ | *Tempo of Consistent Control* | = |

PIECE OR EXERCISE:

Time	Day 1	2	3	4	5	6	7
Improvement							

ideas and feelings

| WEEKLY SUMMARY | *Feelings* ◯ | *Degree of Completion* ◯ | *Stuck Without Teacher* ◯ | *Tempo of Consistent Control* | = |

PIECE OR EXERCISE:

Time	Day 1	2	3	4	5	6	7
Improvement							

ideas and feelings

| WEEKLY SUMMARY | *Feelings* ◯ | *Degree of Completion* ◯ | *Stuck Without Teacher* ◯ | *Tempo of Consistent Control* | = |

PIECE OR EXERCISE:

Time	Day 1	2	3	4	5	6	7
Improvement							

ideas and feelings

WEEKLY SUMMARY	Feelings ◯	Degree of Completion ◯	Stuck Without Teacher ◯	Tempo of Consistent Control	=

PIECE OR EXERCISE:

Time	Day 1	2	3	4	5	6	7
Improvement							

ideas and feelings

WEEKLY SUMMARY	Feelings ◯	Degree of Completion ◯	Stuck Without Teacher ◯	Tempo of Consistent Control	=

PIECE OR EXERCISE:

Time	Day 1	2	3	4	5	6	7
Improvement							

ideas and feelings

WEEKLY SUMMARY	Feelings ◯	Degree of Completion ◯	Stuck Without Teacher ◯	Tempo of Consistent Control	=

AVERAGE DAILY PRACTICE FOR THE WEEK

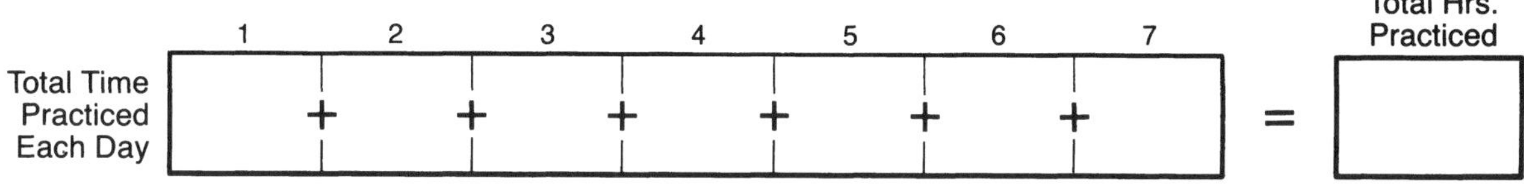

Total Time Practiced Each Day: 1 + 2 + 3 + 4 + 5 + 6 + 7 = Total Hrs. Practiced

Total Hrs. Practiced ÷ Total Days Available = Average Practice Per Day

week 9

PIECE OR EXERCISE:

Time	Day 1	2	3	4	5	6	7
Improvement							

ideas and feelings

WEEKLY SUMMARY	*Feelings* ◯	*Degree of Completion* ◯	*Stuck Without Teacher* ◯	*Tempo of Consistent Control* =

PIECE OR EXERCISE:

Time	Day 1	2	3	4	5	6	7
Improvement							

ideas and feelings

WEEKLY SUMMARY	*Feelings* ◯	*Degree of Completion* ◯	*Stuck Without Teacher* ◯	*Tempo of Consistent Control* =

PIECE OR EXERCISE:

Time	Day 1	2	3	4	5	6	7
Improvement							

ideas and feelings

WEEKLY SUMMARY	*Feelings* ◯	*Degree of Completion* ◯	*Stuck Without Teacher* ◯	*Tempo of Consistent Control* =

PIECE OR EXERCISE:

Time	Day 1	2	3	4	5	6	7
Improvement							

ideas and feelings

WEEKLY SUMMARY	*Feelings* ◯	*Degree of Completion* ◯	*Stuck Without Teacher* ◯	*Tempo of Consistent Control* =

PIECE OR EXERCISE:

Time	Day 1	2	3	4	5	6	7
Improvement							

ideas and feelings

| WEEKLY SUMMARY | Feelings ◯ | Degree of Completion ◯ | Stuck Without Teacher ◯ | Tempo of Consistent Control | = |

PIECE OR EXERCISE:

Time	Day 1	2	3	4	5	6	7
Improvement							

ideas and feelings

| WEEKLY SUMMARY | Feelings ◯ | Degree of Completion ◯ | Stuck Without Teacher ◯ | Tempo of Consistent Control | = |

PIECE OR EXERCISE:

Time	Day 1	2	3	4	5	6	7
Improvement							

ideas and feelings

| WEEKLY SUMMARY | Feelings ◯ | Degree of Completion ◯ | Stuck Without Teacher ◯ | Tempo of Consistent Control | = |

AVERAGE DAILY PRACTICE FOR THE WEEK

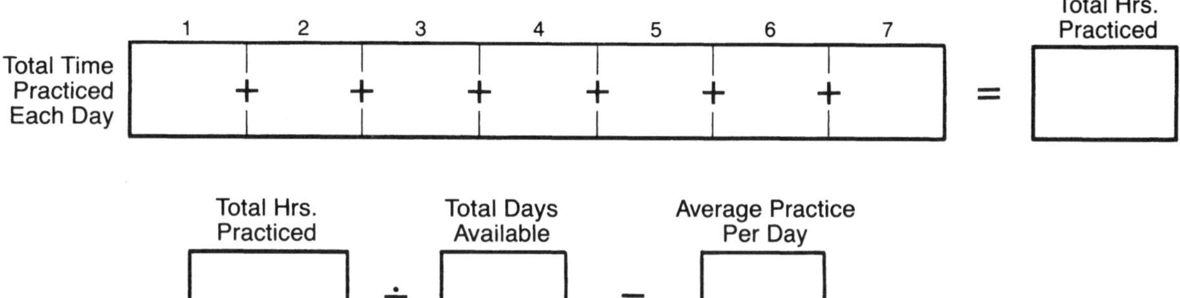

week 10

PIECE OR EXERCISE:

Time	Day 1	2	3	4	5	6	7
Improvement							

ideas and feelings

WEEKLY SUMMARY	*Feelings* ◯	*Degree of Completion* ◯	*Stuck Without Teacher* ◯	*Tempo of Consistent Control* =

PIECE OR EXERCISE:

Time	Day 1	2	3	4	5	6	7
Improvement							

ideas and feelings

WEEKLY SUMMARY	*Feelings* ◯	*Degree of Completion* ◯	*Stuck Without Teacher* ◯	*Tempo of Consistent Control* =

PIECE OR EXERCISE:

Time	Day 1	2	3	4	5	6	7
Improvement							

ideas and feelings

WEEKLY SUMMARY	*Feelings* ◯	*Degree of Completion* ◯	*Stuck Without Teacher* ◯	*Tempo of Consistent Control* =

PIECE OR EXERCISE:

Time	Day 1	2	3	4	5	6	7
Improvement							

ideas and feelings

WEEKLY SUMMARY	*Feelings* ◯	*Degree of Completion* ◯	*Stuck Without Teacher* ◯	*Tempo of Consistent Control* =

PIECE OR EXERCISE:

Time	Day 1	2	3	4	5	6	7
Improvement							

ideas and feelings

WEEKLY SUMMARY	Feelings ◯	Degree of Completion ◯	Stuck Without Teacher ◯	Tempo of Consistent Control [=]

PIECE OR EXERCISE:

Time	Day 1	2	3	4	5	6	7
Improvement							

ideas and feelings

WEEKLY SUMMARY	Feelings ◯	Degree of Completion ◯	Stuck Without Teacher ◯	Tempo of Consistent Control [=]

PIECE OR EXERCISE:

Time	Day 1	2	3	4	5	6	7
Improvement							

ideas and feelings

WEEKLY SUMMARY	Feelings ◯	Degree of Completion ◯	Stuck Without Teacher ◯	Tempo of Consistent Control [=]

AVERAGE DAILY PRACTICE FOR THE WEEK

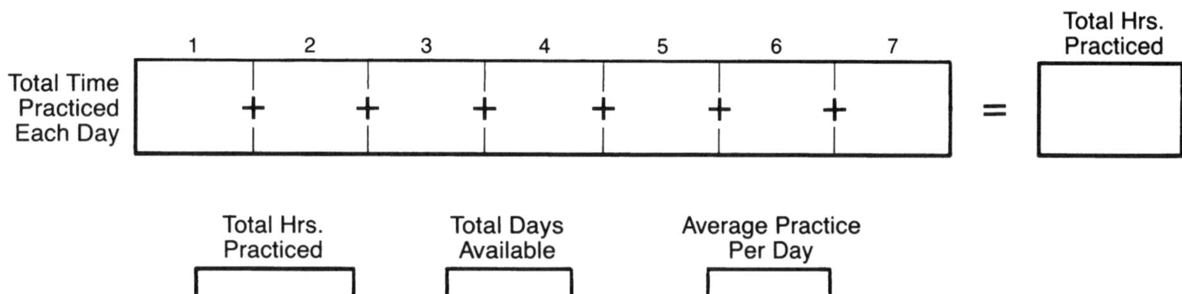

week 11

PIECE OR EXERCISE:

Time	Day 1	2	3	4	5	6	7
Improvement							

ideas and feelings

WEEKLY SUMMARY	*Feelings* ◯	Degree of Completion ◯	Stuck Without Teacher ◯	Tempo of Consistent Control $=$

PIECE OR EXERCISE:

Time	Day 1	2	3	4	5	6	7
Improvement							

ideas and feelings

WEEKLY SUMMARY	*Feelings* ◯	Degree of Completion ◯	Stuck Without Teacher ◯	Tempo of Consistent Control $=$

PIECE OR EXERCISE:

Time	Day 1	2	3	4	5	6	7
Improvement							

ideas and feelings

WEEKLY SUMMARY	*Feelings* ◯	Degree of Completion ◯	Stuck Without Teacher ◯	Tempo of Consistent Control $=$

PIECE OR EXERCISE:

Time	Day 1	2	3	4	5	6	7
Improvement							

ideas and feelings

WEEKLY SUMMARY	*Feelings* ◯	Degree of Completion ◯	Stuck Without Teacher ◯	Tempo of Consistent Control $=$

PIECE OR EXERCISE:

Time	Day 1	2	3	4	5	6	7
Improvement							

ideas and feelings

| WEEKLY SUMMARY | *Feelings* ◯ | *Degree of Completion* ◯ | *Stuck Without Teacher* ◯ | *Tempo of Consistent Control* [=] |

PIECE OR EXERCISE:

Time	Day 1	2	3	4	5	6	7
Improvement							

ideas and feelings

| WEEKLY SUMMARY | *Feelings* ◯ | *Degree of Completion* ◯ | *Stuck Without Teacher* ◯ | *Tempo of Consistent Control* [=] |

PIECE OR EXERCISE:

Time	Day 1	2	3	4	5	6	7
Improvement							

ideas and feelings

| WEEKLY SUMMARY | *Feelings* ◯ | *Degree of Completion* ◯ | *Stuck Without Teacher* ◯ | *Tempo of Consistent Control* [=] |

AVERAGE DAILY PRACTICE FOR THE WEEK

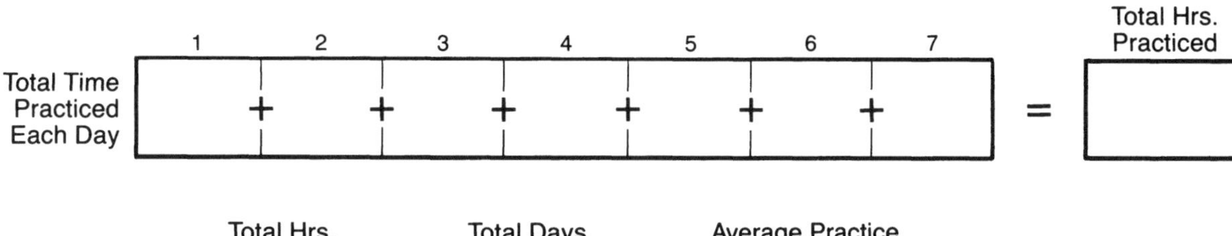

week 12

PIECE OR EXERCISE:

Time	Day 1	2	3	4	5	6	7
Improvement							

ideas and feelings

| WEEKLY SUMMARY | *Feelings* ◯ | Degree of Completion ◯ | Stuck Without Teacher ◯ | Tempo of Consistent Control | = |

PIECE OR EXERCISE:

Time	Day 1	2	3	4	5	6	7
Improvement							

ideas and feelings

| WEEKLY SUMMARY | *Feelings* ◯ | Degree of Completion ◯ | Stuck Without Teacher ◯ | Tempo of Consistent Control | = |

PIECE OR EXERCISE:

Time	Day 1	2	3	4	5	6	7
Improvement							

ideas and feelings

| WEEKLY SUMMARY | *Feelings* ◯ | Degree of Completion ◯ | Stuck Without Teacher ◯ | Tempo of Consistent Control | = |

PIECE OR EXERCISE:

Time	Day 1	2	3	4	5	6	7
Improvement							

ideas and feelings

| WEEKLY SUMMARY | *Feelings* ◯ | Degree of Completion ◯ | Stuck Without Teacher ◯ | Tempo of Consistent Control | = |

PIECE OR **EXERCISE:**

Time	Day 1	2	3	4	5	6	7
Improvement							

ideas and feelings

WEEKLY SUMMARY	Feelings ◯	Degree of Completion ◯	Stuck Without Teacher ◯	Tempo of Consistent Control	=

PIECE OR **EXERCISE:**

Time	Day 1	2	3	4	5	6	7
Improvement							

ideas and feelings

WEEKLY SUMMARY	Feelings ◯	Degree of Completion ◯	Stuck Without Teacher ◯	Tempo of Consistent Control	=

PIECE OR **EXERCISE:**

Time	Day 1	2	3	4	5	6	7
Improvement							

ideas and feelings

WEEKLY SUMMARY	Feelings ◯	Degree of Completion ◯	Stuck Without Teacher ◯	Tempo of Consistent Control	=

AVERAGE DAILY PRACTICE FOR THE WEEK

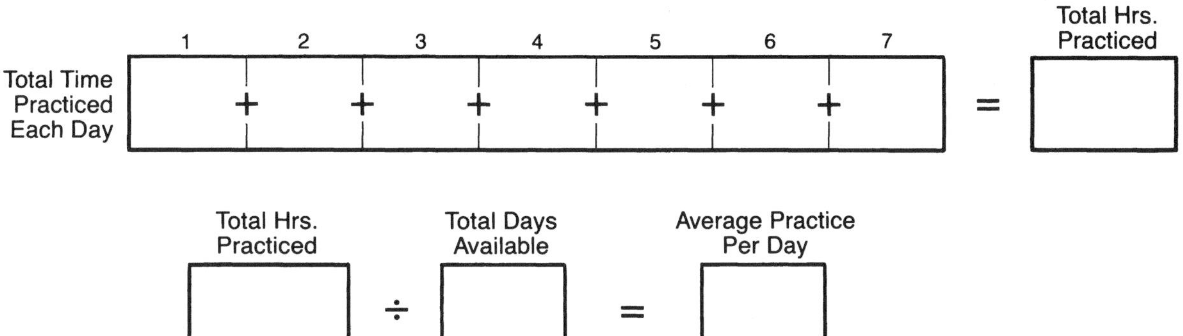

week 13

PIECE OR EXERCISE:

Time	Day 1	2	3	4	5	6	7
Improvement							

ideas and feelings

WEEKLY SUMMARY	*Feelings* ◯	Degree of Completion ◯	Stuck Without Teacher ◯	Tempo of Consistent Control =

PIECE OR EXERCISE:

Time	Day 1	2	3	4	5	6	7
Improvement							

ideas and feelings

WEEKLY SUMMARY	*Feelings* ◯	Degree of Completion ◯	Stuck Without Teacher ◯	Tempo of Consistent Control =

PIECE OR EXERCISE:

Time	Day 1	2	3	4	5	6	7
Improvement							

ideas and feelings

WEEKLY SUMMARY	*Feelings* ◯	Degree of Completion ◯	Stuck Without Teacher ◯	Tempo of Consistent Control =

PIECE OR EXERCISE:

Time	Day 1	2	3	4	5	6	7
Improvement							

ideas and feelings

WEEKLY SUMMARY	*Feelings* ◯	Degree of Completion ◯	Stuck Without Teacher ◯	Tempo of Consistent Control =

PIECE OR EXERCISE:

Time	Day 1	2	3	4	5	6	7
Improvement							

ideas and feelings

| WEEKLY SUMMARY | Feelings ◯ | Degree of Completion ◯ | Stuck Without Teacher ◯ | Tempo of Consistent Control | = |

PIECE OR EXERCISE:

Time	Day 1	2	3	4	5	6	7
Improvement							

ideas and feelings

| WEEKLY SUMMARY | Feelings ◯ | Degree of Completion ◯ | Stuck Without Teacher ◯ | Tempo of Consistent Control | = |

PIECE OR EXERCISE:

Time	Day 1	2	3	4	5	6	7
Improvement							

ideas and feelings

| WEEKLY SUMMARY | Feelings ◯ | Degree of Completion ◯ | Stuck Without Teacher ◯ | Tempo of Consistent Control | = |

AVERAGE DAILY PRACTICE FOR THE WEEK

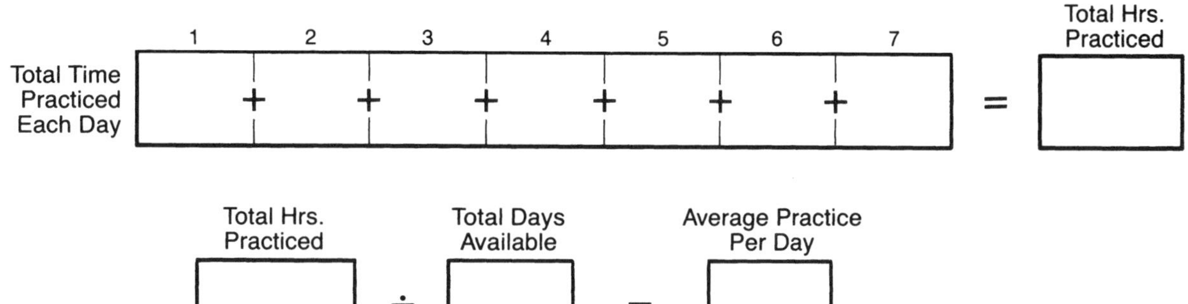

week 14

PIECE OR EXERCISE:

Time	Day 1	2	3	4	5	6	7
Improvement							

ideas and feelings

| WEEKLY SUMMARY | *Feelings* ◯ | *Degree of Completion* ◯ | *Stuck Without Teacher* ◯ | *Tempo of Consistent Control* = |

PIECE OR EXERCISE:

Time	Day 1	2	3	4	5	6	7
Improvement							

ideas and feelings

| WEEKLY SUMMARY | *Feelings* ◯ | *Degree of Completion* ◯ | *Stuck Without Teacher* ◯ | *Tempo of Consistent Control* = |

PIECE OR EXERCISE:

Time	Day 1	2	3	4	5	6	7
Improvement							

ideas and feelings

| WEEKLY SUMMARY | *Feelings* ◯ | *Degree of Completion* ◯ | *Stuck Without Teacher* ◯ | *Tempo of Consistent Control* = |

PIECE OR EXERCISE:

Time	Day 1	2	3	4	5	6	7
Improvement							

ideas and feelings

| WEEKLY SUMMARY | *Feelings* ◯ | *Degree of Completion* ◯ | *Stuck Without Teacher* ◯ | *Tempo of Consistent Control* = |

PIECE OR EXERCISE:

Time	Day 1	2	3	4	5	6	7
Improvement							

ideas and feelings

WEEKLY SUMMARY	Feelings ◯	Degree of Completion ◯	Stuck Without Teacher ◯	Tempo of Consistent Control =

PIECE OR EXERCISE:

Time	Day 1	2	3	4	5	6	7
Improvement							

ideas and feelings

WEEKLY SUMMARY	Feelings ◯	Degree of Completion ◯	Stuck Without Teacher ◯	Tempo of Consistent Control =

PIECE OR EXERCISE:

Time	Day 1	2	3	4	5	6	7
Improvement							

ideas and feelings

WEEKLY SUMMARY	Feelings ◯	Degree of Completion ◯	Stuck Without Teacher ◯	Tempo of Consistent Control =

AVERAGE DAILY PRACTICE FOR THE WEEK

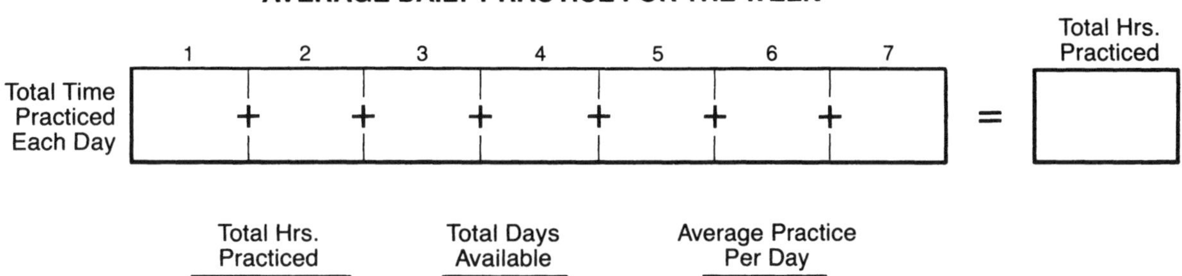

week 15

PIECE OR EXERCISE:

Time	Day 1	2	3	4	5	6	7
Improvement							
ideas and feelings							

WEEKLY SUMMARY	*Feelings* ◯	*Degree of Completion* ◯	*Stuck Without Teacher* ◯	*Tempo of Consistent Control* =

PIECE OR EXERCISE:

Time	Day 1	2	3	4	5	6	7
Improvement							
ideas and feelings							

WEEKLY SUMMARY	*Feelings* ◯	*Degree of Completion* ◯	*Stuck Without Teacher* ◯	*Tempo of Consistent Control* =

PIECE OR EXERCISE:

Time	Day 1	2	3	4	5	6	7
Improvement							
ideas and feelings							

WEEKLY SUMMARY	*Feelings* ◯	*Degree of Completion* ◯	*Stuck Without Teacher* ◯	*Tempo of Consistent Control* =

PIECE OR EXERCISE:

Time	Day 1	2	3	4	5	6	7
Improvement							
ideas and feelings							

WEEKLY SUMMARY	*Feelings* ◯	*Degree of Completion* ◯	*Stuck Without Teacher* ◯	*Tempo of Consistent Control* =

From _________ to _________ 20 __

PIECE OR EXERCISE:

Time	Day 1	2	3	4	5	6	7
Improvement							

ideas and feelings

| WEEKLY SUMMARY | *Feelings* ◯ | *Degree of Completion* ◯ | *Stuck Without Teacher* ◯ | *Tempo of Consistent Control* ⬜ = |

PIECE OR EXERCISE:

Time	Day 1	2	3	4	5	6	7
Improvement							

ideas and feelings

| WEEKLY SUMMARY | *Feelings* ◯ | *Degree of Completion* ◯ | *Stuck Without Teacher* ◯ | *Tempo of Consistent Control* ⬜ = |

PIECE OR EXERCISE:

Time	Day 1	2	3	4	5	6	7
Improvement							

ideas and feelings

| WEEKLY SUMMARY | *Feelings* ◯ | *Degree of Completion* ◯ | *Stuck Without Teacher* ◯ | *Tempo of Consistent Control* ⬜ = |

AVERAGE DAILY PRACTICE FOR THE WEEK

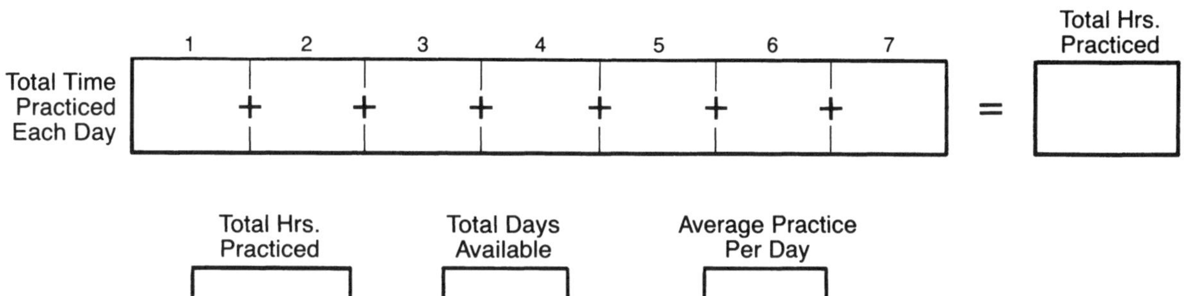

week 16

PIECE OR EXERCISE:

Time	Day 1	2	3	4	5	6	7
Improvement							

ideas and feelings

WEEKLY SUMMARY	Feelings ◯	Degree of Completion ◯	Stuck Without Teacher ◯	Tempo of Consistent Control ⬚ =

PIECE OR EXERCISE:

Time	Day 1	2	3	4	5	6	7
Improvement							

ideas and feelings

WEEKLY SUMMARY	Feelings ◯	Degree of Completion ◯	Stuck Without Teacher ◯	Tempo of Consistent Control ⬚ =

PIECE OR EXERCISE:

Time	Day 1	2	3	4	5	6	7
Improvement							

ideas and feelings

WEEKLY SUMMARY	Feelings ◯	Degree of Completion ◯	Stuck Without Teacher ◯	Tempo of Consistent Control ⬚ =

PIECE OR EXERCISE:

Time	Day 1	2	3	4	5	6	7
Improvement							

ideas and feelings

WEEKLY SUMMARY	Feelings ◯	Degree of Completion ◯	Stuck Without Teacher ◯	Tempo of Consistent Control ⬚ =

PIECE OR EXERCISE:

Time	Day 1	2	3	4	5	6	7
Improvement							

ideas and feelings

| WEEKLY SUMMARY | *Feelings* ◯ | *Degree of Completion* ◯ | *Stuck Without Teacher* ◯ | *Tempo of Consistent Control* | = |

PIECE OR EXERCISE:

Time	Day 1	2	3	4	5	6	7
Improvement							

ideas and feelings

| WEEKLY SUMMARY | *Feelings* ◯ | *Degree of Completion* ◯ | *Stuck Without Teacher* ◯ | *Tempo of Consistent Control* | = |

PIECE OR EXERCISE:

Time	Day 1	2	3	4	5	6	7
Improvement							

ideas and feelings

| WEEKLY SUMMARY | *Feelings* ◯ | *Degree of Completion* ◯ | *Stuck Without Teacher* ◯ | *Tempo of Consistent Control* | = |

AVERAGE DAILY PRACTICE FOR THE WEEK

	1	2	3	4	5	6	7		Total Hrs. Practiced
Total Time Practiced Each Day		+	+	+	+	+	+	=	

Total Hrs. Practiced [ ] ÷ Total Days Available [ ] = Average Practice Per Day [ ]

Weekly and Monthly Reflections
practice profile graphs

Putting in the Time—weekly reflections

PROFILE OF ACTUAL TIME PRACTICED EACH DAY   Date begun _______________

HOURS

6
5½
5
4½
4
3½
3
2½
2
1½
1
½
0

| 1 2 3 4 5 6 7 | 1 2 3 4 5 6 7 | 1 2 3 4 5 6 7 | 1 2 3 4 5 6 7 |
| WEEK 1 | WEEK 2 | WEEK 3 | WEEK 4 |

HOURS

6
5½
5
4½
4
3½
3
2½
2
1½
1
½
0

| 1 2 3 4 5 6 7 | 1 2 3 4 5 6 7 | 1 2 3 4 5 6 7 | 1 2 3 4 5 6 7 |
| WEEK 5 | WEEK 6 | WEEK 7 | WEEK 8 |

Key

------ Total Time Planned
——— Actual Time Practiced

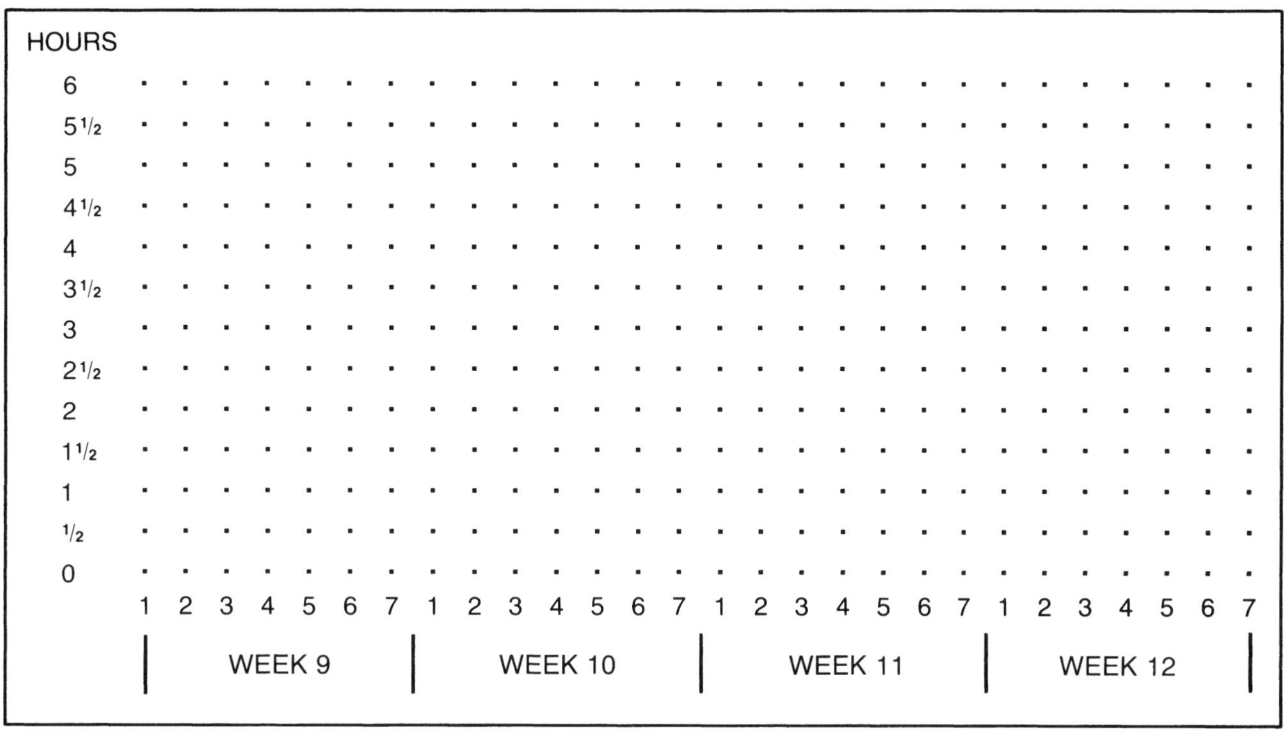

HOURS
6
5½
5
4½
4
3½
3
2½
2
1½
1
½
0
1 2 3 4 5 6 7 1 2 3 4 5 6 7 1 2 3 4 5 6 7 1 2 3 4 5 6 7
WEEK 9
WEEK 10
WEEK 11
WEEK 12

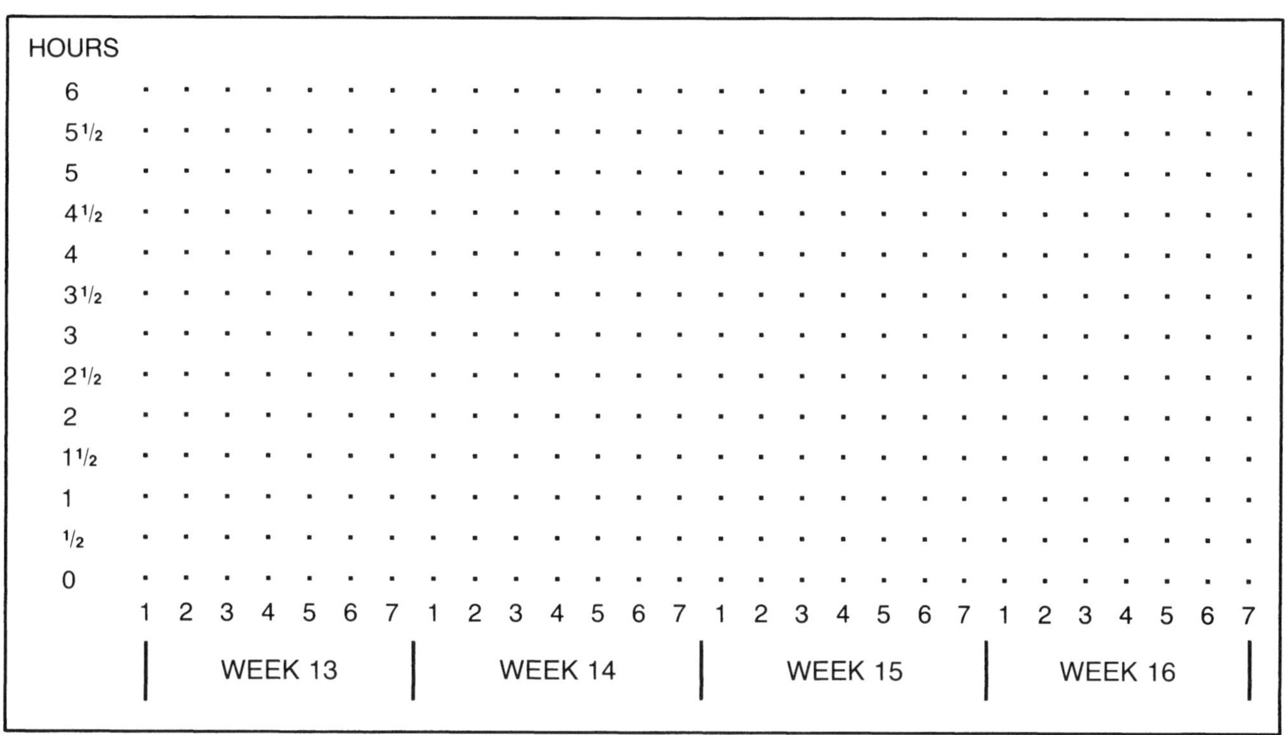

HOURS
6
5½
5
4½
4
3½
3
2½
2
1½
1
½
0
1 2 3 4 5 6 7 1 2 3 4 5 6 7 1 2 3 4 5 6 7 1 2 3 4 5 6 7
WEEK 13
WEEK 14
WEEK 15
WEEK 16

TIME MANAGEMENT PROFILES

1. I practiced (more than, as much as, less than) I planned to.

more than

as much as

less than

WEEK   1 2 3 4 5 6 7 8 9 10 11 12 13 14 15 16

2. This week, I found that my

life and practice schedules balance

practice crowds out life

life crowds out practice

WEEK   1 2 3 4 5 6 7 8 9 10 11 12 13 14 15 16

(If your life and practice schedules do not balance, make a plan to improve the balance and log it in the diary that begins on the next page.)

3. I (am satisfied, am not satisfied) that if I put in each week the amount of time I put in this week, my ambition can be fulfilled.

am satisfied

am not satisfied

WEEK   1 2 3 4 5 6 7 8 9 10 11 12 13 14 15 16

PROFILE OF AVERAGE DAILY PRACTICE EACH WEEK FOR 16 WEEKS

HOURS

6

5½

5

4½

4

3½

3

2½

2

1½

1

½

0

    1 2 3 4 5 6 7 8 9 10 11 12 13 14 15 16

WEEK

Key

- - - - - - Average Daily Time Planned for the Week

———— Average Daily Practice for the Week

55

WK #	DATE	**DIARY OF IDEAS:** *How I can put in more time.*

WK #	DATE	**DIARY OF IDEAS:** *How I can put in more time.*
56		

WK #	DATE	**DIARY OF IDEAS:** *How I can put in more time.*

57

Putting in the Time — monthly reflections

SUMMARY OF MY PRACTICE PROFILE GRAPHS

STRENGTHS   WEAKNESSES

________________________________   ________________________________

________________________________   ________________________________

________________________________   ________________________________

________________________________   ________________________________

Reread your log to date and record additional observations here: __________________________

Check each of the items below which best expresses your attitudes and intentions:

___ I have excellent control of putting in the time.

___ I accept my present level of putting in the time, though it is not good enough to achieve my ambition.

___ I improved in putting in the time this month.

___ I did not follow my plan this month.

___ Last month's plan to improve putting in the time did not succeed.

___ I do not plan any changes this month.

___ I plan the following changes in an effort to improve ___ the amount of time I put in, ___ the regularity of the time I put in:

SUMMARY OF MY PRACTICE PROFILE GRAPHS

STRENGTHS   WEAKNESSES

_____________________________   _____________________________

_____________________________   _____________________________

_____________________________   _____________________________

_____________________________   _____________________________

_____________________________   _____________________________

Reread your log to date and record additional observations here: _______________

____

____

____

____

Check each of the items below which best expresses your attitudes and intentions:

____ I have excellent control of putting in the time.

____ I accept my present level of putting in the time, though it is not good enough to achieve my ambition.

____ I improved in putting in the time this month.

____ I did not follow my plan this month.

____ Last month's plan to improve putting in the time did not succeed.

____ I do not plan any changes this month.

____ I plan the following changes in an effort to improve ____ the amount of time I put in, ____ the regularity of the time I put in: ____

____

____

____

____

SUMMARY OF MY PRACTICE PROFILE GRAPHS

STRENGTHS   WEAKNESSES

Reread your log to date and record additional observations here: ___________________________

Check each of the items below which best expresses your attitudes and intentions:

___ I have excellent control of putting in the time.

___ I accept my present level of putting in the time, though it is not good enough to achieve my ambition.

___ I improved in putting in the time this month.

___ I did not follow my plan this month.

___ Last month's plan to improve putting in the time did not succeed.

___ I do not plan any changes this month.

___ I plan the following changes in an effort to improve ___ the amount of time I put in, ___ the regularity

of the time I put in: ____

SUMMARY OF MY PRACTICE PROFILE GRAPHS

STRENGTHS

WEAKNESSES

Reread your log to date and record additional observations here: _______________

Check each of the items below which best expresses your attitudes and intentions:

____ I have excellent control of putting in the time.

____ I accept my present level of putting in the time, though it is not good enough to achieve my ambition.

____ I improved in putting in the time this month.

____ I did not follow my plan this month.

____ Last month's plan to improve putting in the time did not succeed.

____ I do not plan any changes this month.

____ I plan the following changes in an effort to improve ____ the amount of time I put in, ____ the regularity of the time I put in:

Using Practice Time Effectively—weekly reflections

PRACTICE EFFECTIVENESS PROFILES

1. I feel (fulfilled, satisfied, disappointed) with the overall improvement that has occurred this week.

fulfilled	.	.	.	.	.	.	.	.	.	.	.	.	.	.	.	.
satisfied	.	.	.	.	.	.	.	.	.	.	.	.	.	.	.	.
disappointed	.	.	.	.	.	.	.	.	.	.	.	.	.	.	.	.
WEEK	1	2	3	4	5	6	7	8	9	10	11	12	13	14	15	16

2. As I practiced, I (rarely, sometimes, often) succumbed to distractions.

rarely	.	.	.	.	.	.	.	.	.	.	.	.	.	.	.	.
sometimes	.	.	.	.	.	.	.	.	.	.	.	.	.	.	.	.
often	.	.	.	.	.	.	.	.	.	.	.	.	.	.	.	.
WEEK	1	2	3	4	5	6	7	8	9	10	11	12	13	14	15	16

(If distracted "often" or "sometimes," describe the nature of the distractions — whether they came, for example, *from within* or *from without*. Make a plan now for reducing the distractions next week and log it in your diary that begins at the bottom of the next page.

3. My concentration and attention were strongly focused.

95% +	.	.	.	.	.	.	.	.	.	.	.	.	.	.	.	.
ofton	.	.	.	.	.	.	.	.	.	.	.	.	.	.	.	.
sometimes	.	.	.	.	.	.	.	.	.	.	.	.	.	.	.	.
rarely	.	.	.	.	.	.	.	.	.	.	.	.	.	.	.	.
WEEK	1	2	3	4	5	6	7	8	9	10	11	12	13	14	15	16

4. I paced my work so I did not fatigue easily.

95% +	.	.	.	.	.	.	.	.	.	.	.	.	.	.	.	.
often	.	.	.	.	.	.	.	.	.	.	.	.	.	.	.	.
sometimes	.	.	.	.	.	.	.	.	.	.	.	.	.	.	.	.
rarely	.	.	.	.	.	.	.	.	.	.	.	.	.	.	.	.
WEEK	1	2	3	4	5	6	7	8	9	10	11	12	13	14	15	16

5. I used The Daily Practice Organizer to organize my work each day.

95% +	.	.	.	.	.	.	.	.	.	.	.	.	.	.	.	.
often	.	.	.	.	.	.	.	.	.	.	.	.	.	.	.	.
sometimes	.	.	.	.	.	.	.	.	.	.	.	.	.	.	.	.
rarely	.	.	.	.	.	.	.	.	.	.	.	.	.	.	.	.
WEEK	1	2	3	4	5	6	7	8	9	10	11	12	13	14	15	16

6. Rather than skip around impulsively, I followed my daily practice plan.

| 95%+ |
| often |
| sometimes |
| rarely |
| WEEK | 1 2 3 4 5 6 7 8 9 10 11 12 13 14 15 16 |

7. I practiced each assigned item during each practice day. When I didn't, it was the result of an intelligent decision.

| 95%+ |
| often |
| sometimes |
| rarely |
| WEEK | 1 2 3 4 5 6 7 8 9 10 11 12 13 14 15 16 |

8. I knew or invented a way of practicing each work that produced satisfying results.

| 95%+ |
| often |
| sometimes |
| rarely |
| WEEK | 1 2 3 4 5 6 7 8 9 10 11 12 13 14 15 16 |

9. My expectations and what I achieved coincided.

| 95%+ |
| often |
| sometimes |
| rarely |
| WEEK | 1 2 3 4 5 6 7 8 9 10 11 12 13 14 15 16 |

For each item where your response is not at the highest level, think about how you might improve your work next week and log in your thoughts in the section which begins below.

WK #	DATE	**DIARY OF IDEAS:** *How I can improve my practice effectiveness.*

WK #	DATE	**DIARY OF IDEAS:** *How I can improve my practice effectiveness.*
64		

WK #	DATE	**DIARY OF IDEAS:** *How I can improve my practice effectiveness.*
		65
WK #	DATE	**DIARY OF IDEAS:** *How I can improve my practice effectiveness.*

66		

<table>
<tr><th>WK #</th><th>DATE</th><th>DIARY OF IDEAS: How I can improve my practice effectiveness.</th></tr>
<tr><td></td><td></td><td>67</td></tr>
</table>

Using Practice Time Effectively — monthly reflections

SUMMARY OF MY PRACTICE PROFILE GRAPHS

STRENGTHS   WEAKNESSES

Reread your log to date and record additional reflections here: ______________________

Check each of the items below which best expresses your attitudes and intentions:

____ I am exceptionally effective in the way I use my practice time.

____ I accept my present level of effectiveness, though it is not good enough to achieve my ambition.

____ I improved in using my time effectively this month.

____ Last month's plan to improve how I use my time did not succeed.

____ I do not plan any changes this month.

____ I plan the following changes in an effort to practice more effectively: ______________________

SUMMARY OF MY PRACTICE PROFILE GRAPHS

STRENGTHS   WEAKNESSES

_______________________________   _______________________________

_______________________________   _______________________________

_______________________________   _______________________________

_______________________________   _______________________________

Reread your log to date and record additional reflections here: _______________________

____

____

____

____

____

Check each of the items below which best expresses your attitudes and intentions:

____ I am exceptionally effective in the way I use my practice time.

____ I accept my present level of effectiveness, though it is not good enough to achieve my ambition.

____ I improved in using my time effectively this month.

____ Last month's plan to improve how I use my time did not succeed.

____ I do not plan any changes this month.

____ I plan the following changes in an effort to practice more effectively: _______________

____

____

____

____

____

____

SUMMARY OF MY PRACTICE PROFILE GRAPHS

STRENGTHS   WEAKNESSES

___________________________________   ___________________________________

___________________________________   ___________________________________

___________________________________   ___________________________________

___________________________________   ___________________________________

___________________________________   ___________________________________

Reread your log to date and record additional reflections here: ___________________________________

____

____

____

____

Check each of the items below which best expresses your attitudes and intentions:

____ I am exceptionally effective in the way I use my practice time.

____ I accept my present level of effectiveness, though it is not good enough to achieve my ambition.

____ I improved in using my time effectively this month.

____ Last month's plan to improve how I use my time did not succeed.

____ I do not plan any changes this month.

____ I plan the following changes in an effort to practice more effectively: ________________________

____

____

____

____

____

SUMMARY OF MY PRACTICE PROFILE GRAPHS

STRENGTHS   WEAKNESSES

____________________________   ____________________________

____________________________   ____________________________

____________________________   ____________________________

____________________________   ____________________________

____________________________   ____________________________

Reread your log to date and record additional reflections here: ____________________________

Check each of the items below which best expresses your attitudes and intentions:

____ I am exceptionally effective in the way I use my practice time.

____ I accept my present level of effectiveness, though it is not good enough to achieve my ambition.

____ I improved in using my time effectively this month.

____ Last month's plan to improve how I use my time did not succeed.

____ I do not plan any changes this month.

____ I plan the following changes in an effort to practice more effectively: ______________________

Technique Achievement Summary

SCALES—1ˢᵀ Level of Quality

SCALE																
Memorized Y/N																

REFINING SCALE QUALITY

Key and No. of Octaves	Manner of Execution	Level of Completion					
		Tempo*	Mem. Y/N	Tone Quality*	% Even & Articulate	% in Tune	

ARPEGGIOS—1ˢᵀ Level of Quality

ARPEGGIO																
Memorized Y/N																

REFINING ARPEGGIO QUALITY

Key and No. of Octaves	Manner of Execution	Level of Completion					
		Tempo*	Mem. Y/N	Tone Quality*	% Even & Articulate	% in Tune	

*Tempo = Tempo of Consistent Control

*Tone Quality Code: E = Excellent, G = Good, F = Fair, & P = Poor.

ETUDES

Composer and Opus	Etude No.	Level of Completion						
		Tempo*	Mem. Y/N	% of Rhythmic Control	Phrasing Dynamics Expression	Tone Quality*	% in Tune	

OTHER TECHNICAL EXERCISES

*Tempo = Tempo of Consistent Control

*Tone Quality Code: E = Excellent, G = Good, F = Fair, & P = Poor.

Repertoire Achievement Summary

Concertos: Mem.*   Level of Completion*

	Mem.*	Level of Completion*

Sonatas: Mem.   Level of Completion

	Mem.	Level of Completion

Other Pieces: Mem.   Level of Completion

	Mem.	Level of Completion

Orchestral Excerpts: Mem.   Level of Completion

	Mem.	Level of Completion

*Level of Completion: RTP = Ready to Perform, Perf = Performed   *Mem: Y = Memorized
TPTL = To Present Technical Level   N = Not Memorized
EFN = Enough for Now
CSIAM = Can't Stand It Any More

Record of Performances

Piece	Date	Occasion and Type of Performance*	Degree of Satisfaction

*Type of Performance: Solo, Orchestral, Chamber Music Concert,
Competition, Performance Class, Audition

Guide to Types of Practicing

Guide to Types of Practicing and General Strategies for Practicing

Practicing is most satisfying when it is methodically organized, not haphazard. You should be precise about what you are trying to improve, i.e., rhythm, tone, intonation, interpretation, phrasing, projection, use of your body, etc. And, above all, you should be precise about how you will go about making your improvements. When you can describe how you will go about making an improvement, you have a strategy. An effective strategy is a procedure which leads directly to your increasing control of the music. Often your teacher will prescribe a strategy to help you practice effectively. However, you should try to invent your own when you do not feel the strategy you are using is paying off.

Keep in mind that a strategy is a consciously directed procedure. If you cannot write it down or describe it out loud, you do not have a strategy. When you find that you are playing without a specific strategy in mind, stop! If you do not know an appropriate strategy and you cannot invent one, check the "stuck without teacher" box in your Daily Practice Log and make a note of where you need help and the kind of help you need. Then go on to practice something else. The guide below will help you define the type of practicing you should be doing and give you ideas for strategies that you can use to increase your practicing effectiveness.

Types of Practicing	**General Strategies**
A. Learning New Repertoire	1. Sight-read through many times with a musical attitude — get the feel of the entire work.
	2. Play through to mark problem areas (sections, phrases, spots).
	3. Develop consistent control of problem areas.
	4. Integrate improved problem areas into larger sections, and then into the whole work.
	5. Turn your attention to interpreting and expressing the music. Stop paying attention to technical control.
B. Restudying Old Repertoire	1. Play through musically, several days in a row, to bring the piece back to life.
	2. Play through to decide what needs the most attention.
	3. Improve your control of the parts which need the most attention.
	4. Integrate newly refined parts into the whole work.
C. Learning a New Skill	1. Define how to use your body. Attend to — degree of effort, timing, rhythm, selection of movements, direction of movements.
	2. Define the sound. Attend to — rhythm, tone quality (intensity, articulation, volume, beauty), and intonation.
	3. Integrate effective use of body with desired sound.

D. Refining an Old Skill

1. Refine the way you use your body. Attend to—degree of effort, timing, rhythm, selection of movements, direction of movements.

2. Refine the sound. Attend to—rhythm, tone quality (intensity, articulation, volume, beauty), and intonation.

3. Integrate refined use of body with desired sound.

E. Warming Up

Experiment until you find a routine that makes you feel alive and ready to make music. In other words, warm up your mind and your spirit, not just your muscles. Here are some strategies to try:

1. Sight-read to get in the mood. Begin with a piece that reflects your present mood.

2. Begin with a different piece or exercise each day.

3. Begin with the same piece or exercise each day.

4. Begin with stretching and calisthenic exercises. Keep in mind that playing a musical instrument is a physical activity.

5. Listen to a tape recording of your work from the day before.

F. Maintaining Your Skill Level

On the days when you have little time available to practice, do not try to improve or learn repertoire. Be satisfied to go through your warm-up routine and sensitize yourself to each of the priority works you have been practicing. You will then be ready to continue work where you left off the next time you practice. You will not have lost ground.

G. Preparing for a Performance

In a performance, you get only one try. Test your performance during your practice by playing through only once (no second chances). Your first try play-through during your practice is close to what you can expect when you perform.

H. Getting Back Into Shape

1. If you have not played for a while, practice slowly, and for short periods at first. Your system needs to get used to playing again gradually.

2. Stop the first moment any part of your system begins to feel fatigue. Rest! Then continue.